apostrophe

apostrophe

compiled by
Bill Kennedy and Darren Wershler-Henry

MISFIT

Bill Kennedy and Darren Wershler-Henry have not accepted royalties for
this work. All royalties from the sales of this book will be donated to Creative
Commons Canada, a nonprofit organization funded entirely by grants and
public donations.

The publication of apostrophe has been generously supported by the Canada
Council, the Ontario Arts Council, and the Government of Canada through the
Book Publishing Industry Development Program.

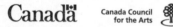

LIBRARY AND ARCHIVES CANADA CATALOGUING IN PUBLICATION

Kennedy, Bill, 1969 –
    Apostrophe / Bill Kennedy and Darren Wershler-Henry.

"A misFit book".
Poems.
ISBN 1-55022-722-X

    1. Canadian poetry (English) – 21st century. I. Wershler-Henry,
Darren S. (Darren Sean), 1966- II. Title.

PS8621.E63A68 2006   C811'.608   C2006-900477-3

ECW PRESS
ecwpress.com

Build an engine with words. Let it make you speak.
– Steve Venright

apostrophe (ninety-four)

you are a deftly turned phrase, an etymological landscape, a home by the sea • you are a compilation of more than 60 samples overlaid on top of a digitally synthesized '70s funk groove • you are the message on a cassette tape long after it has been recorded over • you are, as such, the eraser head's self-validating ideal of order • you are a festering war wound incurred in a skirmish between the US and Canada over rights to a pig farm strategically located on what is now referred to as the world's longest unde-fended border, making you a better meteorologist than any one of the "big three" networks, or the CBC for that matter, can muster • you are used and abused • you are a distress property bought by Tom Vu and sold for an outrageous profit • you are ossifying sweat on Robert Plant's performance towel, now in the possession of a man who is thinking about auctioning it off because he has decided he would rather listen to "new country" • you are an onion ring with an identity crisis on the Korona Restaurant's "Transylvanian Meat Platter" • you are an easy-riding H that just knew you would be stopped by police, cuffed, hauled in and strip-searched while you were making your way through the mountains in Georgia • you are everything your mother had hoped for and more • you are track lighting gone bad, a one-time energy saver now driving a gas-guzzling '71 Impala • you are considering touching that dial • you are a pretense to universality • you are the top quark • you are one of a family of Dirt Devil carpet cleaners • you are wondering at this moment whether you are merely a cleverly disguised rip-off • you are a foreign agent who acciden-tally ruptured an emergency cyanide tooth cap just before your rendezvous with a thin man in a lumber jacket standing by a garbage can on the patio of a McDonald's in Paris, who was to receive an attaché case containing vital information photo-reduced on microfilm, which, of course, you have no prior knowledge of • you are a mispronounced word with eyes stuck in an awkward position just like your parents warned you they would, trying to get a date with one of the "cool chicks" in your high school and having a difficult time of it • you are fibre ingested by a septuagenarian to promote regularity • you are a face in the crowd • you are secretly responsible for both the mysterious circles appearing overnight in British grain fields and getting the soft-flowing caramel into the Caramilk bars • you are not using the Force, Luke • you are fucked up in your own special way • you are toiling, neither do you spin • you are your own secret twin preparing to make an appearance on *Ricki!* • you are an immediately perceptible phenomenon elevated to the level of theological unity • you are accurate to a depth of 30 m • you are pecs on your pecs • you are thrown out for lack of evidence • you are a nested loop • you are getting sleepy • you are an ode to the west wind • you are made in your own image • you are wanted and loved … as if • you are a case of halitosis, gingivitis, dandruff and split ends all rolled up into one • you are a granny knot undone by an older and wiser scout leader • you are a piece of performance art that deep down inside wants to be a bust of Beethoven sitting on a Steinway grand piano • you are a primal scream trying to differentiate yourself from an existential scream • you are a hockey stick broken over the spine of a 19th century hunchback you figured had no business playing street hockey in the first place • you are a healthy Hi-Pro glow • you are having paranoid delusions that a figure much like Henri Matisse's *Blue Nude* is following you around trying to get you to join the Jehovah's Witnesses • you are the distance between the hyperbolic curve at the y-axis • you are what you eat • you are a reified universal transcendental signifier • you are kind of pissed off that you were never given the choice of whether to be a sequitur or not • you are and if you aren't, who is? • you are not enough to get over the threshold • you are getting even sleepier • you are a fine piece of work, you are • you are a stupid English k(o)n-ig(g)ht • you are currently in search and destroy mode • you are a 60-cycle hum • you are a refutation of the Special Theory of Relativity • you are a parade of endless details • you are the lusts of your father • you are wondering at the audacity of some people who like to tell you just who they think you are • you are synaptic information lost in the aphasic shuffle • you are a means of production • you are the line cut out of the final edit by some guy using a PowerBook in a cheesy local Laundromat, or if you aren't you wish you were • you are being completely irrational • you are the wrong answer on the multiple choice section of the LSAT • you are feeling quite overwhelmed, you must say • you are exactly what they've been looking for and that should frighten you • you are the significant answer in an inkblot test • you are well on your way • you are the space between the heavens and the corner of some foreign field • you are rendered completely useless • you are a B- grade on a C paper • you are so beautiful, to me • you are unconsciously acting upon your cultural biases • you are a game of tic-tac-toe that, after dealing with an inferiority complex, beat up a game of "global-thermonuclearwar" and kicked the shit out of Pentagon computers • you are on your way to the store to get a litre of milk, when this cow with the head and antlers of a moose sporting a black eye patch over his left eye comes up to you and says "you are on your way to the store to get a litre of milk, when this cow with the head and antlers of a moose sporting a black eye patch over his left eye comes up to you and says '"you are …"'" • you are the weak argument in an elaborate doctoral thesis • you are the miracle cure for halitosis, gingivitis, dandruff and split ends all rolled up into one, at least that's what your 19th century procurer, "Dr. Morgan," says as he travels from town to town trying to sell you • you are not but let's say you are • you are your favourite letter of the alphabet except H cuz that has already been taken • you are an asshole (ee-o-ee-ole) • you are a soliloquy on a barren heath in a play that inspired Shakespeare's *King Lear* but has been lost for many centuries, last documented in the Earl of Derby's private collection in 1723 • you are billed as the "nicotine patch to the world" • you are everything you want in a drugstore • you are only as good as the next guy • you are the eggman, you are the eggman, you are the walrus (goo goo a' joob) • you are shovelling shit in a Roman stable • you are dead now, so shut up! • you are in the process of being palimpsested • you are an incestuous mess • you are available only through this limited TV offer • you are the party of the first part • you are a no-good, lazy son of a bitch • you are often replaced by an apostrophe • you are a big waste of time, for the most part • you are a poor player who struts and frets his hour upon the stage and is heard no more • you are surely mistaken • you are a detachable penis • you are therefore you think • you are the side effects of performance-enhancing drugs • you are a bad case of blue-balls • you are boldly going where no man has gone before, but only as the disposable crew member who happens to be dumb enough to talk to a lump of painted grey Styrofoam and therefore, in my humble opinion, deserves to get it anyway • you are translated into 20 different languages • you are not smart, just hard working • you are a painting bought solely for the frame • you are the only one who really likes it, really • you are not a machine, you are a human being • you are corn, but we call it maize • you are dumb enough to spend your time typing out endless statements that begin with "you are" just to make a point and try to get some laughs, neither of which, in retrospect, you believe you will succeed in • you are the owner of the secret decoder ring and as such have a right to be president of the club • you are the interest accrued overnight by some clever electronic banking maneuver • you are and if you aren't you should be • you are misspelled in a grade six spelling bee by a kid who will eventually serve eight years in jail for manslaughter • you are better than bad, you're good • you are a quote within a quote desperately trying to escape • you are a most noble swain • you are in absentia • you are engaging in self-nullifying behaviour • you are a vague sense of alienation masked by a friendly, conversational atmosphere • you are a dentist, you take delight in causing great pain • you are the kind of apathy that can only be generated by the "spoken-" vs. "written-" word debate • you are a self-consuming artifact • you are an unimportant stanza in an unimportant Bob Southey epic • you are the neurochemical dopamine bridging the gap between the tail of one synapse and the head of another during a bout of particularly raunchy sex with a not-quite-loved one • you are an instance of pre-emptory teleology • you are living in a post-theory, post-language writing, post-sound-poetry, post-literate age, so let's stop writing crap that pretends that you aren't • you are a reference to the small font size of this poem • you are going to sell out the first chance you get • you are yawning – stop it! • you are a persnickety line removed at the friendly request of an editor who thinks its potential offensiveness is enhanced by the mere fact of its referential obscurity • you are all out to get me, damn you! • you are mixing memory with desire • you are sitting with a soggy ass at some reading in High Park really wishing you were somewhere else • you are a portable Greek reader that is going to party like it's 1999 • you are going on with your doggy life • you are the interplay between the quotidian and the extraordinary • you are a ravenous carnivore who lusts after the feeling of animal blood tracing the crevasses of your chin, or if you aren't, you know one • you are a captain's log, supplemental • you are a metonymic slide • you are a pipefitter with a penchant for Descartian ontology • you are everyday people • you are believing this crap they're feeding you • you are convinced you looked better before the makeover • you are a bird, no, wait, you are a plane, no, hell! you're Superman! • you are an uninterrupted series of dots that hasn't come to terms with being a line yet • you are an ill-used neural cluster removed to get at a deep-seated brain tumour • you are fading away when you would rather be burning out • you are a linguistic trap set to catch some good eatin' possum •

you are eleven benevolent elephants • you are damp semen
currently stringing its way to the centrefold of a porn mag • you
are a registered trademark of the Coca-Cola corporation • you are
the supreme arbiter and lawgiver of music • you are woman, hear
you roar • you are never going to amount to a hill of beans in the
world • you are bad advice foisted on some lovesick puppy • you
are an axiom proved false • you are the cruellest month • you are
an error in grammar identified by the latest in word-processing
technology • you are flown to your destination on Delta Air Lines
• you are the book in the spirit machine • you are a dadaist who
needs to love and be loved • you were pre-conceived by both
Boethius and William the Conqueror yet still have no clue as to
what surrealism is really on about • you are hoping that you will
never have to hear that fucker read his damn "you are" poem
again but are resigned to that fact that you probably will • you are
in more closets than you wish to admit • you are someone with
the debilitating habit of cutting against the grain • you are going,
going, gone • you are a likely consumer of rubber nipples • you are
a long-lost jazz score that no one would have played anyway • you
are a last will and testament • you are an unceremonious exit

layer two

(a deftly turned phrase)

you are a regular man-eater, do you know that? • you are a devoted matricidal maniac who has decided it is impossible to write about your mother – how she brought you up and how she died – without sentimentality • you are an educator or school organization such as a PTA • you are a bard then, not a warrior? • you are a brute • you are a party leader • you are a prophet – our fathers worshipped in this mountain • you are a mere computer • you are a mere computer • you are a bit battered at the moment • you are a true intellectual, I will have to give you a more comprehensive answer than most • you are a lover of gold jewellery • you are a vegetarian so I suggest going to the Eden Restaurant • you are an American coming to Greece for an extended period of time • you are a tourist with a fairly old tube map, or you last came to London over five years ago and you may be wondering what happened to Aldwych tube station • you are a fan of Dark Funeral, Marduk and Setherial, but don't like the Peter Tagtgren studio sound • you are a rap artiste, emcee, like the late Richard Dawson, not to be confused with the periodic table of elements • you are a minor and/or offended by such things, go watch Public Television RIGHT NOW • you are a metaphor for God • you are a teacher who has begun to suspect that a child is being bullied at school • you are a Berkeleian idealist or a realist • you are a genuine talent, Mister • you are a lost woman who will betray everything for what little power you think you desire • you are a man, you have no guest right here • you are a curious one • "You are a reincarnated soul of many past lives," Vivian was relaying with astonishment • you are a junior or senior in high school and this movie was made for you so run and check it out • you are a true romantic, you believe in the power of love and you are willing to take a leap of faith so this movie is for you • you are an insomniac and you like cool, dark places so go see this movie • you are a young person who has not seen many movies and you might (emphasis on might) enjoy yourself • you are a regular moviegoer so you have seen all this before • you are a *Star Trek* fan so I would not discourage you from going to see this movie (not that I would have success) and I guess you will enjoy it • you are a Matthew Perry fan (it's ok; you don't have to be ashamed, sir) – save your money because he basically plays the same character as in *Friends* (which you can watch for free on tv) • you are a liberal Christian who has drifted away from many biblical teachings so your inclination to join social activist groups is understandable • you are encouraged to give SchoolNotes • you are a disgrace to every scientist, every inventor, every person who has ever tried to improve the status of mankind by demonstrating that which they allege • you are an artist, are you not, Mr. Dedalus? said the dean, glancing up and blinking his pale eyes • you are a reactionary then? • you are an Irishman but your pride is too powerful • you are a distressing pair, you and Cranly • you are a child of God • you are a foreigner, I'll swear, because you have such a fine contempt for us • you are a unique being, spiritual as well as physical and in spite of the terrible enigma of unexplainable evil – part of an essentially harmonious universe • you are a monster • you are a genius • you are a friend, I cannot simply release you without hard proof of your innocence, not in dangerous times like this • you are a great Orientalist • you are an Esperantist • you are a restless sleeper • you are a guest here; and we – I – will respect your reticence about our customs • you are a Yorkshire girl too? • you are a skilful pilot, Robert • you will weather the storm • you are a Jacobin • you are a peculiar personage: quiet as you look, there is both a force and a depth somewhere within, not easily reached or appreciated • you are a Whig or a Tory: pray which party has the honour of your alliance? • YOU ARE A FLUKE OF THE UNIVERSE • YOU HAVE NO RIGHT TO BE HERE; AND WHETHER YOU CAN HEAR IT OR NOT, THE UNIVERSE IS LAUGHING BEHIND YOUR BACK • you are a teacher, are you not, as well as a pupil? • you are a scoundrel • you are a sort of Swiss sibyl, with high Tory and high Church principles! • you are a more unpractical man than I am an unpractical woman, for you don't acknowledge what really exists • you are a fool and that I am a worse fool yet

(an etymological landscape)

you are told it only seem'd or looked that way, but wasn't really •
"you are my master and my author" • you are told it only seem'd
or looked that way, but wasn't really • "you are my master and my
author" • "you are my guide, my governor, my master" • you are
looking for a listing of libraries and this is a great place to look •
you are going to visit and want to know about the weather, where
to eat, where to stay and what to do • you are looking • you are
really depressed and you just want to shout "SHUT UP! SHUT UP!
SHUT UP!" • you are not behind the project to the extent that we
require • you are 27 so you are a Gen-Xer • you are much more in
touch with your personal process • you are in it for the money •
you are surrounded by people who take the lazy route • you are
carrying the battle standard and don't know it • you are not really
graduating • you are nothing to me • you are my absence from
your life • you are not me! • you are describing a moment of
change • you are playing with time and rhythm • you are skeptical,
gentle reader • you are already finding out I'm neither • you are
starting to cost me real money! • you are wondering again: Jackson
Browne? But hey, when you write these sorts of penetrating and
insightful business books for busy executive types, you take your
inspiration wherever you find it • you are told that "shut up" is not
that different a proposition from "shut up and buy our product" •
"you are writing a book," he drawls • "you are not writing it!"
Weinberger thunders • you are not alone in this southern desert;
love, like a wounded elephant, terrible and pathetic, storms the
deadly streets to hunt us down • you are not so lucky today,
rehearses the other, the guilty animal; look at tomorrow – the
good days are gone and in the future, everything you do will go
wrong and you will be broken down

(a home by the sea)

you are nose-to-nose with one long, sharp shark snout • you are
of no interest at all • you are hopelessly lost • you are heading
across a hot, dry desert covered with sand dunes • you are head-
ing across a grassy plain • you are unsure where you are going or
what you are going to see along the way but you'll know once you
get there • you are going to make a dream come true • you are
going, but I'll bet you end up somewhere else • you are a fool to
waste your time reading any further • you are smart enough to do
it now and you will, I promise, be one step closer to your dream
than if you don't • you are invited to write it down simply because
writing it down is a shortcut • you are living your dream life of
passion, excitement, fun, service and productivity so by all means
continue • you are not getting it from the horse's mouth, so at
which end of the horse will we find you? • you are a first-time
angler, a weekend warrior or a seasoned salmon pro who desires
to perfect his fishing knowledge and Salmon University will teach
you the intricacies of catching some of the most awe-inspiring
fish in the sea • you are interested • you are interested in "Puget
Sound south" • you are ready to go fishing, or you have a question
• you are at a party with a blind date and he starts making lewd
gestures and crude comments • you are not impressing anyone •
you are the one for him • you are here: home > TV shows > tech
news > culture > now you're cooking with tech • you are tired of
burning your finger while checking the temperature of your
secret sauce, so stop!

(a compilation of more than 60 samples overlaid on top of a digitally synthesized '70s funk groove)*

you are in for some good head • you are my personal angel and peaceful • you are a budding funk miner/crate digger looking for great blistering funk and you leave no stone unturned • you are splashing out some cash • you are a completist • you are not a fetishist • you are still feeling this urge • you are welcome stop on by, Lyn Collins was on here with (think about it) one of the most sampled songs in history, listen to it and folks 25 and over will agree with me, "Take Me Just As I Am" is the bomb Maceo on sax took me to funkland, then we want to party I love how Lyn sang that at the end, another sax solo by Maceo, those are my favourite tracks on this double CD if you love James Brown and want to hear how some of his best divas sounded this is for if you can't get enough of Maceo Parker and Fred Wesley this is for you though I recommend the JBS horns, and the JBS doing it to death • you are the sunshine of my life and more • you are satisfied • you are in town! • you are here don't forget to • you are like me, you buy even if it means eating beans on toast for a week! • you are expecting a rehash of the heavy jams that burned on the dap dippin' album, you won't be disappointed, but get ready for a deep, natural (hence the title soulfulness) that not only caught us off guard, but really forms the big, hard-beating heart of it • you are my sunshine • you are the one for me/edited version

(the message on a cassette tape)

you are signed up and you can begin • you are ready to play the game • you are represented by a little astronaut figure which can be moved around the screen with a joystick • you are required to bring a letter with you on your first visit • you are motivated • you are sincere • "you are sincere" is saying "as long as you are already pure in your intentions, you are right to believe anything you wish" • you are going to hear from a fellow by the name of Peter Sun • you are looking for a great opportunity and you have found it! Peter Sun tells it like it is! He is a master at direct marketing! • you are looking for a missionary or friend who needs the latest sermons and raps, or perhaps have a family member that will enjoy listening to sermons • you are given hypnosis to help correct your specific problems • you are too busy to write your own script so take advantage and let us do the work

(a self-validating ideal of order)

you are driving along on H1 minding your own business, then suddenly you glance in your rear-view mirror and see some fucking idiot trying to read a bumper sticker that you don't have on your bumper • you are going 45 in a 55 mph zone • "you are upset that I'm late for dinner, but is there more about that?" your partner might respond by saying something like: "yes, I am and there is more! I'm tired of keeping dinner warm until you get home" • you are angry about that and I can imagine that you might also feel hurt and betrayed • you are going to be late, so call me thirty minutes before you planned to come home and when you come bring me a single yellow rose • you are actually safer when you lower your defences than when you keep them engaged, because your partner becomes an ally, not an enemy • you are feeling all those symptoms, but what does your body want to do? Does it want to scream? Does it want to hit? Does it want to cry? Does it want to love? Does it want to hide? • you are in crisis • you are searching for your license, so it must be within reach • you are frustrated and the primitive impulse is to destroy the figure that did the hurt • you are going to kill and destroy a part of me that's already dead to you now • you are reliving the old event, but you don't just simply relive it as it was and then stop • you are asked to role-play and you say "I will role-play the negative aspects of your father or mother" • you are asked to say "I never wanted you to be born" • you are role-playing or accommodating and making all the sounds of pain • you are asked to play the ideal figure • you are 80 years old and looking back • you are vibrating • you are holographic • you are including yourself in that picture • you are contemplating aligning with your higher self and this is what causes the excitement • you are "meant" to be doing – what your soul "hopes" your will free will chooses to do • you are likewise changing your past and your future • you are shifting to a totally different hologram that contains its own "past" that is consistent with its "present" and also its own "future," which is likewise consistent with its "present" • you are granting equality and validity to all aspects of creation and as a reflective result of this, the entire creation supports you in everything you do as well! • you are attracting that reality • you are not attracting that reality • you are all you have to work with in your universe • you are the representation, in your own way, of the infinite • you are attracting into your reality the very thing you "believe" you need to be protected from • you are not a great parent or you suck everyone dry or you put others second • you are writing gibberish • you are composing more than decomposing • you are, like most people, spending a disproportionate amount of time worrying about the effort that went into its content • you are finally done

(a festering war wound incurred in a skirmish between the us and Canada over rights to a pig farm)*

you are reading this, and I'm almost certain that you are: you need to trim that *Cat in the Hat* piece by about a third • you are going to miss the not-so-subtle reference • you are probably free of head injury • you are scrunching over in an effort to make more room for your neighbour • you are wasting your talents on overly obvious targets – don't limit yourself to mocking poor white trash, branch out to mocking wealthy white trash – may I recommend the festering eyesore that is Plano, Texas – the wealthiest suburb of Dallas – go check it out, you'll see what a Southern Babtist does with $200,000 a year to blow on ostentatious display! • you are looking for a solutions architect who's worked as an architect at Telus for Accenture where he was Lead Architect for the it Governance Center Lead Architect for the Borland Caliber rm Application Architect for the iWay Server Architect for smis Solutions Architect/Capacity Planner for Rogers Shared Services now Rogers Shared Operations Solutions Architect/Senior Unix Engineer for rim Senior Architect for YoYoDyne Infrastructure Architect Systems Engineer for Opensoft • you are trying to do that, see if you can wrap your head around this • you are hit, but unlike a paintball, a pellet cannot bounce off • you are not familiar with the term, but it is the name for the four weeks leading up to Christmas • you are considering that the person to collect the cash should also be good with basic mathematics • you are an adventurer, there are 4x4 safaris and some of the best terrain in the world for quadding, moto-X and enduro • you are Canadian – thank God • you are over-qualified • you are now on a 30-day performance plan • you are black • you are moving into check • you are clean-shaven • you are out

(used and abused)*

you are in the middle of a police encounter, you need a handy and quick reference to remind you what your rights and obligations are • you are innocent • you are going to file a complaint • you are injured, take photographs of the injuries as soon as possible, but make sure you seek medical attention first • you are detained or arrested, with one important exception • you are arrested anyway • you are stopped for questioning • you are subsequently asked to identify yourself, see paragraph 2 above • you are under arrest • you are given a ticket, you should sign it; otherwise you can be arrested • you are suspected of drunk driving and refuse to take a blood, urine or breath test • you are arrested, the police can search you and the area close by • you are in a building; "close by" usually means just the room you are in • you are being lied to and everything you know is wrong • you are looking for earth-shattering news, this is not the book for you

(a distressed property bought by Tom Vu and sold for an outrageous profit)

you are the next victim • you are its ambassador and I promise to come to the party you give • you are right and you want the people downstairs to believe and to understand you • you are separated from them and you are mine or if not then you belong to Nebuchadnezzar (king of Babylon) and his comrades • you are in exile, so be distinguished with mitzvot, place tefillin phylacteries and make mezuzot on your doorposts so that they will not be foreign to you when you return • you are crossing the Jordan to drive out the inhabitants of the land from before you as it is written in Numbers 33:52 • you are not an advocate of criminal activity • you are right on top of this kind of violation • you are prepared to defend yourself • you are going to cause a significant serious effect on the life of another by actions such as this • you are required to be in your own residence each day • you are not to be within 500 feet of this address • you are to deal with Revenue Canada by correspondence only unless you are contacted by an official or employee of Revenue Canada for a personal meeting in which case you will be permitted to go on the premises • you are not in the habit of attending any worship services on Sunday mornings • you are not to initiate any contact directly or indirectly with Rod Peltonen or any member of his family • you are fine • you are required by law to report to a sentence supervisor within 48 hours of today • you are the only one I'd want mounted above my fireplace • you are falling into the same habits of stereotyping that you seem to be so angry at Americans for practicing • you are a complete ass! • you are admitted into our august presence as American citizens • you are selling something that it is best to appeal to the lowest common denominator • you are expressing your opinions when spouting off en masse at a protest or whatever • you are not an advertiser, you are a teacher • you are all wrong • you are not an advocate of criminal activity • you are right on top of this kind of violation • you are prepared to defend yourself • you are reading a page put up by some other people who do not appear, in my opinion, to have anything to say • you are not an advocate of criminal activity • you are right on top of this kind of violation • you are approached by this man be prepared to defend yourself • you are not wanted 'cause no one wants a fucktard like you in their country unless they are from south of the border, so go ahead in your little shitbox of a car and putt-putt down to Customs • you are able to verbally bash your own country • you are all wrong • you are up and ready to run • you are getting naked • you are looking for her DVDs and other videos and will find all the best are at Goliath Films • you are using a condom but you sucked a dick without a condom • you are a dumb, yeast-infected fuckpig who thought you could come in, make demands and show a major attitude • you are not interested in something that's all me, for real, my words, my feelings and thoughts, pictures of me at home, in the bathroom, sleeping in bed, showing exclusive photo shoots that no one else has • you are working four, five times a week • "you are saying there is a lot of glucose, as in sugar, in male semen?" "That's correct," responded the professor, going on to add statistical info • you are going to leave and while there may be 50 ways to leave your lover, there are only 4 ways out of this airplane • you are travelling with more than one small child • "you are married or what, Brian?" Brian: (laughing nervously) "Yes, I'm married" • you are off to Orlando, Florida, at our expense • "you are released?" The patient thinks for a moment, then replies "Well, I went to school for mechanical engineering" • you are a brave man • you are Kevin actually seeing the light bulb going off over the customer's head • you are saying that you are the boy's father • you are wanted for destruction of government property, among other charges • you are finally getting your chance to confront me, or your father, who never cared for you • you are hanging out with a bunch of lowlife smugglers and guerrillas, acting like a rebel and busting up stuff throughout the galaxy • you are going to have to face the fact that some of the truths we all hold dear are true • you are concerned that the chicken crossing the road reveals your underlying sexual insecurity • you are full of shit so you may qualify for the supervisory or training position, either giving shit to fellow employees or training others to take shit • you are the seeds and school is the soil • you are having trouble getting started • you are going to forward something so at least send me something mildly amusing • you are actually contributing to the problem • you are as ugly as a hat full of arseholes and have to realize that a friend is someone who cleans up for you after you've soiled yourself, someone who stays with you all night while you cry about your sad, sad life • you are heterosexual • you are feeling particularly blonde today • you are the dog but some days you are the hydrant • you are in the bathroom • you are bad • you are gonna love Mondays then • you are already dead, remember? • you are dead anyhow • you are dead – who cares! • you are really gonna hate Fridays • you are not a member of their religion so you will go to Hell • you are in danger of, say, falling from a large building • you are too far away from the Earth's gravity • you are standing on the Moon holding a pen and you let go • you are standing on the Moon and holding a rock and you let it go • you are gonna say "I wish that sucker would've tried that stuff with me!" • you are blonde and pretty and realize that it is possible to become a world expert in nuclear fission at age 22 • you are not cooking for guys or dogs, so you should use a more elaborate "gourmet" type of recipe, which you can find in magazines such as *Bon Appétit* (literal translation: "chow down") • you are progressing briskly through the steps and suddenly you come across an instruction that the gourmet chef obviously dreamed up moments before passing out face-down in the béarnaise sauce, such as "caramelize eight minced hamouti kleebers into a reduction of blanched free-range whelk corneas" • you are supposed to get shot with an arrow or something, but the rest of it isn't supposed to be so painful • you can last a long time •

you are trying to hide from it • you are proud to be seen in public with your partner • you are only interested in doing things with your partner • you are only interested in doing things to your partner • you are only interested in your golf score • you are running around naked scaring the kids • you are still a little confused • you are a Jurassic geezer • you have the ugliest dork I've ever laid eyes upon • you are hung over • you are really not going to like it • you are dead • you are a woman and you are reading this, which brings up another point: women never listen either • you are going to want to shoot it • you are never too old or too young for chocolate • you are having chocolate and it doesn't keep the neighbours awake • you are never going to get it or how long it is going to last • you are thinking • you are in a gay church and only half the congregation is kneeling • you are looking through bottom of an empty glass • you are being carried out • you are being taken to another bar • you are drunk, Churchill, and Bessie, you are ugly • you are better informed than all of Parliament • you are paying me too much money • you are having flies • you are being killed or you've lost a very important part of your life • you are eager to meet people who do • you are in like Flynn • you are not part of the solution, you are part of the precipitate • you are open 24 hours • you are rocking in a rocking chair and you go so far that you almost fall over backwards but at the last instant you catch yourself • you are trying to think • you are making other plans • you are only six inches away • you are cross-eyed and have dyslexia; can you read all right? • you are harbouring a fugitive: Hu Yu Hai Ding; an illegal execution: Lin Ching; a lighting fixture used in advertising signs: Ne Ahn; a great achievement of the American space program: Moon Lan Ding; a bashful person: Shai Gai; a premature infant: Tai Ne Bae Be; there is no reason to raise your voice: Wai U Shao Ting; serving drinks to people: Ten Ding Ba • you are so full of shit • you are validating my inherent mistrust of strangers • you are an artist • you are trying to get your four-year-old to switch to decaf • you are doing reasonably well, but still have too little going on in your life • you are entitled to receive $$$ • you are paying too much for the AT&T virus • you must now be retyped • you are planning an assassination of Leonardo DiCaprio, just to be sure that those *Episode II* rumours will never come true • you are sure that your 20-year hunger strike is the only thing that convinced George Lucas to write *Episode I* • you are late for work • you are bilingual and can now speak fluid Dwarven • you are not absolutely comfortable • you are not absolutely comfortable with me • you are missing one single peanut and the store personnel will laugh in the chilling manner exhibited by Joseph Stalin just after he enslaved eastern Europe • you are lying the plug on the floor so do not hold a sharp object in your other hand and trip over the cord and poke your eye out as this could void the warranty • you are above average • you are the pioneer type and hold most people in contempt • you are a genius • you are quick-tempered, impatient and scornful of advice • you are a prick • you are practical and persistent • you are stubborn and bull-headed • you are nothing but a Goddamn Communist • you are a quick and intelligent thinker • you are a bisexual • you are inclined to expect too much for too little • you are a cheap bastard • you are sympathetic and understanding to other people's problems • you are a sucker • you are always putting things off • you are pushy • you are vain and cannot tolerate honest criticism • you are the logical type and hate disorder • you are cold and unemotional and often fall asleep while screwing • you are the artistic type and have a difficult time with reality • you are a male and are probably queer • you are shrewd in business and cannot be trusted • you are a perfect son of a bitch • you are optimistic and enthusiastic • you are always getting fucked • you are conservative and afraid of taking risks • you are inclined to be careless and impractical, causing you to make the same mistakes repeatedly • you are a fucking jerk • you are Harry Mathews, or you are being followed by the FBI or CIA • you are the dear old dad of mine? But you cut my hand off and left me to die! Oh Vader, you can't do this to me, Vader, I know there's some good, I know there's still some good in you, may the Force be with you, use the Force to see, may the Force be with you, may the Force be with you, alwaaaaaaaaaaaaaaÿs; anywhere the Force goes, doesn't really matter, to meeeeeeeeeeeeeeeee … to-o me

(ossifying sweat on Robert Plant's performance towel)*

you are not from Portland; visit for the festival, but don't stay • you are having a bad race, just quit • you are walking through a very strange forest or landscape, his music can be rather trippy • you are attempting to do our great city a service • you are living in now • you are going, be sure to wear your "A woman's place is in the House and Senate" T-shirt • you are afraid of the man and hate paying those outrageous electric bills • you are just fucked • you are going to be angry with anyone, be angry with me, but I understand if you didn't like it and I apologize • you are catching the hella pre-big time during a short stint on the West Coast • you are a little distressed at the extra hair you find in the shower drain after you shampoo, I mean, you are only thirty, you can't be going bald yet, right, I mean I guess Uncle Bud never had much of a crown, but you got your hair and your build from your mother's side of the family anyway, and they all have thick heads of hair well into their 70s, I mean except for Pawpaw, but he had that nervous thing when he was a guard at the penitentiary, so that doesn't count • you are still cool-ass • you are unfaithful to me • you are right, they are soooo awesome, I forgot to jizz all over these liner notes/this review/this mp3, since that seems to be all anybody listens to these days • you are such a freak • you are trying to accomplish too much in life • you are like us here at TMT, it's pretty easy to guess what you were doing last week • you are for by the spectroscopic Ken I know that you are hydrogen big whirls have little whirls that feed on their velocity; and little whirls have lesser whirls, and so on to viscosity • you are unfamilar with Anacortes, Washington's artistic epicenter, the Department of Safety, so maybe some handy-dandy information would help you appreciate the wonderful space • you are I've studied your size and I've measured your mass you're not a diamond you are just hydrogen gas physics [top of page] [bottom of page] • you are forced to express sentiments that remove any choice on my part • you are moving and space-time gets "warped" around you;

warping makes the pull • you are a runner and I am my father's son, declaring two and a half minutes of pure grace • "you are not!" Heather insisted • "you are going to another party" she said • "you are going to catch me, okay?" "Uh" • you are womblike and warm • you are all "Whoa" • you are dying to know my opinion on everything, right? Me too! Last night, oh man, I was so tired • you are with me I'm smiling give me, whoa-oh, all your love your hands build me up when I'm sinking touch me and my troubles all fade okay, that was actually written by Styx, but still, you get the idea • you are holding hands and smiling at each other and you know that you are in love, well, it's nice • you are just wantonly throwing them together? For shame • you are not really the person to be heading up the Hoboken office • you are a Christian youth minister, trying to bring the word of the Lord Jesus, not Krishna, to un-salvationed youths? It's hard enough force-feeding the Bible to these blind teens, with their drinking of alcohol, their fornicative fornication, their lust and their greed for material possessions clink-clink goes my gold chains, but now the shepherds have to decipher this unintelligible slang that our children are using in the streets • you are free to invent and they're free to invent and you are neither one hampering the other – that's a very pleasant social form • you are dancing when tears of pain and happiness blend in with your sweat – anonymous – you can dance anywhere, even if only in your heart • you are on thin ice you might as well be dancing • you are there • you are over 35 anyway • you are ecstatic and in love, you feel buoyant, you feel life, you feel like you are dancing in the sky

(an onion ring with an identity crisis on the Korona Restaurant's "Transylvanian Meat Platter")*

you are male, you like a clubby atmosphere, you like your meat well hung, and you are spending $100 of someone else's money • you are somebody • you are a mixed-media god • you are bored with minimalistic architecture and uncluttered decor • you are insulated from it • you are a chess player, you will probably get a good game here • you are not careful, they'll go flying across the room! • you are looking for exotic Vietnamese specialties, you can't beat a dong • you are left with a bog-standard experience

(an easy-riding H that just knew you would be stopped by police)

you are in a new area where the franchises start repeating them-
selves • you are actually on the correct route • you are invited to
the Palais de Justice, 13ème chambre 13h30 on November 17th •
you are an American, you have an attitude and if you have an ego
you don't want to be seen riding foreign junk • you are asking not
for death but for immortality • you are now 200 km out on the
ride instructions and it is easier to follow the map/instructions •
you are going to a French island where they either ask "where's
that?" or laugh • you are just curious to watch the video, so come
along on Thursday, May 18 to Bicycle NSW, Castlereagh Street,
Sydney • you are carrying some food on board even though it may
be a supported ride • you are here on the map that says that the
water and toilets are over by the tennis court • you are interested
in producing an issue so please contact the address above • you
are in a new area where the franchises start repeating themselves

(everything your mother had hoped for and more)[†]

you are pregnant • you are pregnant! what a plus to know you are not the only one who feels fat and unattractive because you are bloated • you are the type who thinks your pregnancy is so special, so sacred, or so precious that having a few laughs about the changes in your body will upset you • you are looking for an interminable discussion of chairs and lighting • you are a Crock-Pot master and are really looking to shake things up • you are old, old and you shall wear your trousers rolled • you are drawn in to the extent that it is hard to imagine that this man did not live and you are convinced to the extent that you believe he probably has, because the author has such a wonderful depth of understanding for the uniqueness of each person's experience of life • you are going to remember me this time • you are wrong • you are boring and totally ordinary and you know it • you are one twisted fuck • you are smoking pot now • you are fucking psycho-boy on a regular basis now? Tell me, has he got a big dick? And don't tell me it's not like that • you are a total prostitute • you are this pampered little suburban chick • you are Goddamn Christy Turlington! I am so sick of people taking their insecurities out on me • you are part-ners, so, uh what's your business? Right, you don't have one • you are the only one who's sexually frustrated here? I'm not? Well then come on, baby, I'm ready! • you are going to turn into a real bitch, just like your mother • you are frightened because you knew, really immediately, that she was right • you are into politics and you want to see how to change bankruptcy law to your own advantage • you are looking for advice for numero uno • you are here • you are pregnant?! • you are the victim of pregnancy discrimination • you are as productive and committed to your job as ever, thereby addressing a perennial fear of many employers • you are suffering from severe morning sickness • you are too full to eat any more

(driving a gas-guzzling '71 Impala)

you are going to help pull our country through this time of tremendous testing! • you are a bit lean and may want to consider richening the calibration up by two percent to be safe • You are a good teacher, Larry, even though you cancelled due to illness • you are a Firebird fan • you are a scout • you are a part of me • you are a "Member Of" COVA/CVAG • you are a part of the problem • you are a part of the problem, re: "You are a part of the problem" (17 lines) • you are a boring, pasty-faced load • you are a cutie, pretty much self-explanatory (found it on a Camaro) • YOU ARE A TOTAL POMPOUS ASS and opening yourself to a lawsuit • you are an egoistic asshole • you are a great person • you are an authority on Chevy II • you are a true Nova fan • you are a pretty cleaver guy • You are a true rod enthusiast • you are a musician that lives on the western slope of Colorado and likes to play music that fits under the category of world music, whatever that means • you are a person of integrity, so the program will continue and the CASH that so many others have received will come your way • you are a mean drunk, or like to fight when you get drunk, so do us all a favour and stay home • you are an American and know that it says right on the passport that it is illegal to photocopy, but the potential hassle for doing so is miniscule compared to the major hassle of having to have your passport replaced when you have a 6 am departure scheduled • you are a western female and are looking for an escort so you should absolutely call an escort agency • you are a PSA guy and realize that this pack should yield some drop-dead MINT cards • you are a hero • you are a very talented poet • you are a little psycho but you're semi-normal • you are a culinary genius • YOU ARE A DISGRACE TO THE BOWTIE F-BODY ROCKS LOS ANGELES – Monday, January 10, 2000 at 22:15:05 (EST) • you are a little infected finger that was affected by disease and must be cut away • you are a member of the ANC, the African National Congress • you are a parent and you leave a house or a home, knowing that the home can survive, because after the death of the old man, the sister also died • you are a family • you are a genius • you are a jealous God? I thought you had everything • you are a Christian and you believe in God even though you wonder what has that got to do with anything • you are a fucking amazing car-maker! This Porsche is perfect, it looks like it could have been a photo of one! Great shading, detail and smoothing and looks just like the real thing – cool

(considering touching that dial)

you are probably gathering from the way I'm phrasing this that I'm trying to say that such a thing invariably opens up a huge minefield of clumsy or inappropriate wording • you are a special individual • you are something! You're a person! You're flesh and blood and bones and hair and nails and ears! You're not a fish! You're having an attack of excited butterflies today; your mind is speeding and you're feeling a little hyper internally though not externally • you are the sort of person who sometimes indulges in the pastime of people-watching, so I can't recommend the Hammersmith bus terminus highly enough • you are really lucky because you can play at avoiding being mown down by one of them as they zoom around on Rollerblades • you are thinking of organizing a party in the near future so you need the perfect act to entertain the guests: "It is now possible to witness electrifying and comedic live performances by Elvis Presley and Marilyn Monroe – together again for the very first time – in the same body! Marvel at the wonder, as Marilyn's sultry voice breathes out Elvis' hit songs, complete with pelvic gyrations, crimson lip curls and giddy "Boop-boop-ee-doo"s! Backed by the irrepressible Botielus on accordion and sequencer, this is one show like no other!" • you are overcome with an insane urge to read through the entire weekly archives from start to finish • you are feeling generous for no particular reason other than the wish to bestow some fluffy brightness on this corner of the world, I hasten to add • you are very observant so you might recognize this stunning panoramic vista from the BBC weather forecasts • you are as excited by that fact as I am • you are using this word about a person, so you are in fact calling them a prostitute – well, in 19th century parlance anyway • you are supposed to say "It's going round, you know" at this point • you are very, very lucky • you are an eagle on the wind, a diamond in the rough, a rare and precious thing • you are the music in my soul, a painter's finest parchment, a poem from the heart • you are a true and timeless friend, a smile that never questions, a love that never ends • you are the one that takes my hand and tells me all I have to do is wish upon a star • you are a fire that's burning bright that keeps me from the cold and warms me through the night • you are my reason to believe that love is all that life can be • you are familiar with any of the more recent Samsung phones, such as the 6100, 8500, etc. • you are a female and you find that your makeup is always getting all over your existing cellular phone and you'll have a real hassle with keeping this screen clean • you are mounting fingerprints on slides • you are concerned about pressure • you are faced with Roger Peters, senior manager of the integrated technology solutions group • you are vulnerable

(a pretense to universality)

you are eating • you are shopping at Wal-Mart • you are eating •
you are shopping at Wal-Mart • you are writing and you must
assume that the next thing you put down belongs there not for
reasons of logic, good sense or narrative development, but
because you put it there • you are writing, so glance over your
shoulder and you'll find there is no reader • you are moved by
water on days like these, so screw him • you are welcome in the
secret club they have formed • you are taught at your daddy's knee
• you are pulling off crooked and dishonest business deals, even
though the Bible says they will all be naked and open to the eyes
of Him to whom we must give account • you are doing evil and it
may be done under the cover of darkness • you are a respectable
sinner because you didn't commit any of those gross sins, but you
are selfish, greedy and critical inside • you are breathing out your
last, and one and only one thing counts • you are clinging to
things you don't want to surrender? • you are giving me a sign of
your love tonight! • you are coming back off that high, high diving
board and kneeling by the side of the pool and saying "Jesus, I'm
making a decision for you" • you are filling out your card, so listen
to Manuel sing this first verse and after the first verse, we'll collect
the cards • you are in the world • you are doing something right
when someone says "I'm surprised" • you are noticing that in fact
there is no exact match • you are related but not the same • you are
here, so why don't you say hello • you are physical with issues of
spirituality • you are headed and if you go to war then that's where
you are headed • you are going and that is not your ultimate goal
• you are talking about, played out in a different way, what I call
"Creativity III" • you are talking about the place where these
famous people became anonymous in their universality • you are
a valuable member of a society that is neurotic • you are that we
ever were – functional • you are familiar with a small book by
George Steiner called *In Bluebeard's Castle* • you are re-instantiating
the very same state of mind the artist is working so hard to get you

out of • you are dealing with material that is violently conflictual, as I think is the case in our culture, then what you are going to end up creating will have a conflictual cast • you are in my head, as all my students are in my head • you are talking about 16th century Europe, where basically the medieval scholastic model had collapsed and you had this enormous ferment for about a century • you are painting it • you are trying to prolong it for as long as you can • you are walking all the time, studying how that affects perception and consciousness • you are not involved in self-deception, so that's what you try to do • you are Ludwig Wittgenstein, or someone who looks a lot like him • you are talking about how you'd like to be able to get society to go in that direction which also has a utilitarian flavour, no? • you are opening the door to the Antichrist and you will face this reality on the day of the judgment seat of Christ! (Church apostasy alert addition: watch for new sections in this book, coming soon) you are Starkitty, but does that not make you Starcat's little sister? • you are not logged in • you are trying to contact me • you are here and you have photos • you are not logged in • you are comfortable with good error-handling idioms and you can quickly learn to use exceptions well • you are bored of me whining about ClearCase, so I'll defer that at least for a couple of days • you are not doing it right • you are not logged in • you are a quick learner and have a good feel for various languages but I would recommend learning the basics from elsewhere • you are writing so you must own a copy of this book • you are interested in writing so this is the book to own • you are a novice writer looking for algorithms and this book has plenty • you are just dabbling like I am, so you should get this book! • you are a fan of Hajime Sorayama, so this is definitely a collection to get • you are not familiar with Hajime Sorayama, so you should know that he's an airbrush illustrator who specializes at least in this volume in the sensual female form combined with technology • you are planning to run away and play, but it's exciting to bring along a friend • you are travelling with rams so let them pick the place and be ready for lots of activity • you are headed out, so let them fling some of their things around the hotel room to make it feel like home, see and pack an extra case for the teddy bear • you are looking to live like royalty, so go with a Leo • you are booking tickets far in advance for the dream trip of a lifetime and you want to lock in a solid itinerary, so book your trip when Mercury is not retro and choose a date of departure when Mercury will not be retro and also when the Moon is not void, of course • you are sending some Wedgwood to Uncle Nigel but realize that you are safer if you deliver it yourself (those packages will rattle just a touch too much otherwise) • you are carrying a pack weighing 100 pounds • you are cold and it's always best to wrap a hot towel around you • you are middling at the skills you choose to have • you are conversational at level VII and a native speaks at level X • you must (yes, must!) forget about

44

global objects • you are not the addressee, so dissemination, copying or other use of this text or any of its content is strictly prohibited and may be unlawful • you are not the intended recipient so please inform the sender immediately and destroy this text and any copies

(one of a family of Dirt Devil carpet cleaners)

you are an old village toymaker and wished upon a star and you will have a boy not of flesh, but of wood and are either withholding me and my fellow seniors of their diplomas unless their parents, relatives or friends pay admission in order to compensate the European shepherd's fee for providing actual sheepskins suitable for framing, flavouring stew or ticking off members of PETA or you are withholding the seniors' diplomas unless they all sign a consent form hereby agreeing to submit themselves to security, not to mention bomb-sniffing dogs whose Gaines Burgers and cans of Cycle 3 are paid for by wacky DJs who know that if any lethal beach balls are hidden under their ceremonial robes, the actual concern should be focused on the possibility of a completely different kind of ball that may appear during the momentous event • you are no better than the people themselves • you are dealing with an audience consisting of people who still envision their graduating children on the day of their birth and you realize you'll get even more presents; sparkly presents so even more really, really cute boys will notice (and maybe they'll give you presents, too!) and are now looking at the mortarboards the graduates are adorning on top of their stupid or shallow or stupid and shallow heads: some have Beanie Baby lions pinned on top of them and some have messages written on them with the aid of first aid tape regarding that bad guy in *Dick Tracy* and you don't want everyone to think you are related to that bad guy in *Dick Tracy*; you want everyone to think you are related to Madonna in *Dick Tracy*, which now feels uneasy because Madonna's into spanking and spanking's really, really really bad unless you are a brain who manages a grunge musician so she can get out of graduation and let her pretty and popular cousin get her diploma so she can spank the grunge musician she manages after the grunge musician's band that she manages finish performing at some other school's graduation party, a party where there'll be dreamily really, really really cute guys who'll notice what you are wearing and they'll give you sparkly presents so really, really really cute guys at another school who has a graduation party will notice and they'll give you sparkly presents too • you are a pretty and popular girl who eats carrots 'cuz if you are a pretty and popular girl who eats carrots, your eyes will be all sparkly and all the guys will notice how sparkly your eyes are, but if all the guys know that a pretty and popular girl wore striped underwear, they'll all think that a pretty and popular girl's really, really slender 'cuz striped underwear's really, really, really slenderizing • you are getting older if you remembered 11-15 = don't tell your age, Darlene • you are ridin' ahead of the herd, so take a look back every now and then to make sure it's still there • you are a person of some influence, so try orderin' somebody else's dog around • you are full of bull, so keep your mouth shut • you are throwin' your weight around, so be ready to have it thrown around by somebody else • you are right and the Bible's not true – so you can do what you want to do • you are gone and it doesn't matter what you've done wrong • you are dead, you are dead • you are wrong, you've got reason to dread, for you are lost in your sins and Hell lies ahead!

(merely a cleverly disguised rip-off)*

you are the unquestioned mistress of the blog • you are going to
drink and you have a social host who'll "watch" stuff • you are
going to get busted and you had better do it right! • you are gonna
do something wrong so ya gotta do it the right way and be sneaky
• you are gonna be bad so do it the right way and be sneaky! and
I had to go to a corner so as no one else would be struck by the
lightning, gotta watch out for the best interest of the others • you
are currently signed in as nobody • you are young, but that's OK –
what's give-or-take nine years anyway? – from "Rock Me" – Liz
Phair burst onto the scene in the mad Chicago band grab of early-
mid-'90s • you are in any doubt about his abilities, I refer you to
this list, with iTunes/Amazon links for easy listening • you are
only looking at the market surface of it – but that's your problem
• you are going to subject us to a lengthy and totally unnecessary
scene of full-frontal nudity from your annoying female lead, you
ought to make up for it by having your very attractive male lead
at least take his Goddamn shirt all the way off once • you are scary
• you are suspicious of an offer, it's usually with good reason • you
are trying to use one basic essay for several different applications
• you are still reading, at least

(a foreign agent who accidentally ruptured an emergency cyanide tooth cap)*

you are an adult, go ahead and read it • you are going to post about a complex legal issue like electronic eavesdropping on foreign agents where domestic contact with said agents is possible; you might want to – instead of using a child's view of the issue as a hammer to beat your political opponents with – take a reasoned look at it prior to knee-jerking a response • you are denied boarding because there are too many passengers for the seats available, an airline must first ask for volunteers to give up their seats in return for agreed benefits • you are mugged, give up whatever you are asked to • you are familiar with them • you are in public and you start experiencing these symptoms, first ask yourself, did anything out of the ordinary just happen, a loud pop, did someone spray something on the crowd? Are other people getting sick too? Is there an odour of new-mown hay, green corn, something fruity, or camphor where it shouldn't be? If the answer is yes, then breathe calmly – if you panic, you breathe faster and inhale more poison – leave the area and head upwind or outside • you are clean of person and home; you eat well and are active • you are joking here • you are damn right I would have done anything to have stopped the brutal carnage wrought upon innocent civilians; it may be disgusting to you, but it was heartbreaking for me to watch a friend, with his face half-blown away, racked with pain and dying as he drowned in his own blood • you are damn right • you are probably gonna live • you are probably going to live • you are all hypnotized

(a mispronounced word with eyes stuck in an awkward position just like your parents warned you they would)

you are convinced you are about to blow off with a resounding trumpeting noise in a public place and all that actually slips out is a tiny "pffft" • you are carrying the load and are getting steadily longer • you are desperate to go to the lavatory and the person you are talking to keeps on remembering a few final things he wants to mention • you are stretched out sunbathing • you are going to have to spend half an hour with a safety pin trying to pull the drawstring out again • you are Andy Stewart • you are driving and the kids are making you a nervous wreck • you are definitive • you are supposed to know what it is • you are talking to someone with your mouth full of half-chewed bread crumbs or small pieces of whitebait • you are slightly smutty postcards from Ibiza getting pinned up by snitterbies • you are not wearing a jacket • you are not drunk • you are trying to get away from the most boring person at a party • you are trying to treat them perfectly casually and normally, but find to your horror that your conversation is liberally studded with references to (a) Long John Silver, (b) Hopalong Cassidy, (c) the Hokey Pokey, (d) "putting your foot in it," (e) "the last leg of the UEFA competition" • you are said to have committed a wigan • you are tired • you are something that differs from what is described here, so tell me about it; and if I think it's important to do so, I'll note that fact • you are right, I'll correct it; but be prepared to be disagreed with • you are being deliberately paradoxical • you are making the object of the adoption your own, accepting it • you are changing it • you are in agreement • you are sure to be branded as uneducated • you are being direct and unambiguous, because you refer to the subject rather than alluding to it • you are speaking of "every other" as in "our club meets on alternate Tuesdays" • you are ambiguous, not ambivalent • you are ambivalent about it; but if you have no particular feelings about it, you are indifferent • you are counting glasses • you are eager for or looking forward to a happy event • you are not sure whether a noun ending in "s" should be followed by an apostrophe, so ask yourself whether you could plausibly substitute "his" or "her" for the "s" • you are really saying "automated teller machine machine" when you say "ATM machine" • you are a jock? One way to impress them is to pronounce "athlete" properly, with just two syllables, as "ath-leet" instead of using the common mispronunciation "ath-uh-leet" • you are a dolt; by all means, mix them up • you are at peoples' beck and call, which means they can summon you whenever they want: either by gesture (beck) or speech (call) • you are not comfortable with formal terms of logic, so it's best to stay away from this phrase, or risk embarrassing yourself • you are writing in psychology, sociology, anthropology, or a related field and it is better to avoid the use of "behaviours" in your writing • you are referring to the Jewish Bible, the Torah, plus the prophets and the writings, or the Protestant Bible – the Jewish Bible plus the New Testament – or the Catholic Bible, which contains everything in the Jewish and Protestant Bibles plus several other books and passages mostly written in Greek in its Old Testament, so the word "Bible" must be capitalized • you are talking about people who should be ashamed of themselves • you are a motel operator offering a different brand of whirlpool bath in your rooms, so you better not call it a "Jacuzzi" • you are viewing the movement of something from the point of arrival, so use "bring": "When you come to the potluck, please bring a green salad" • you are speaking literally of the tough build-up on a person's hand or feet, so the word you need is "callused" • you are on your own, so I suggest you use the final comma • you are not certain a comma is required, so read your sentence aloud • you are stressing similarities between the items compared, so the most common word is "to," as in "She compared his homemade wine to toxic waste" • you are not making nice to someone, so the word is "complement" • you are being complimentary • you are trying to sound a bit more formal • you are taking a bigger risk when you use it to mean "utterly wipe out" • you are writing for a British publication, so use "defence," even though the American "defense" has the advantages of greater antiquity, similarity to the words from which it was derived and consistency with words like "defensible" • you are experiencing a sensation of déjà vu • you are threading your way through troubles as if you were traversing a dangerously narrow passage • you are in "dire straits" • you are drunk • you are trying to render dialectical speech to convey a sense of down-home rusticity, so use "dragged" as the past tense of "drag" • you are using dye to change your favourite T-shirt from white to blue so you are dyeing it; but if you don't breathe for so long that your face turns blue, you may be dying • you are talking about the effect of some measure on the world's economy • you are a lawyer • you are more likely to have a use for ellipses when quoting some source in a paper: "Ishmael remarks at the beginning of *Moby Dick*, 'some years ago'" • you are feeling empathy • you are feeling sympathy • you are envious of your boyfriend's CD collection • you are getting longer

(fibre ingested by a septuagenarian to promote regularity)*

you are a *chica* – 25 grams • you are a *chico* – 38 grams • you are ready to go! • you are going to fail • you are miserable while you're cleansing, you are probably cleansing too fast and should decrease the amounts of the most active ingredients in your cleansing program • you are looking for something gentle yet effective • you are not gaining enough or gaining too much • you are sure to find some helpful information, interesting tips and hints, and articles that address the most common concerns • you are making some great choices already and you should feel good about that • you are in a mid-afternoon slump • you are always assured that they only use live insects

(a face in the crowd)

you are dead!! [to Kurama: you've recovered from your wounds? Kurama: I will have you by tomorrow] • you are hurt, it's normal • you are too stupid for that • you are realizing that you are going to lose • you are feeling really hot and sweaty and uncomfortable • you are not wearing anything underneath so you can't exactly take your shirt off • you are quite happy with your facial features, but lately your nose has really been getting you down • you are in a business environment • you are Asian; you can dress in a suit • you are the high-end guy • you are not around and they'll say to their jelly buddies "Check out the marmalade boy" • you are one of the berries, so you are pretty cool • you are just a cheap hybrid but you can fool them for a time • you are one of those kids that get those "special" education classes in school • you are counting on everything being the same as when you were single last time, but forget it • you are going to have to get out and find out what's going on, find out where you are at • you are going to have trouble keeping up let alone passing yourself off as a teenybopper • you are probably not quite ready for the nursing home either, so if you are going to do any good, you are going to have to mess with Mr. X • you are bitter and hostile and the rest of us singles aren't going to be too enthused or happy about meeting you either • you are going down for two hours of fun • you are drinking – and can fill a beer can with soda • you are a child of the universe • you are either with America or against us • you are being lied to and it will blow your remaining neurons to smithereens • you are able to sleep at night • you are on a boat and your boat is sinking, so you hang your flag upside-down • you are reading it now, so no need to hype it! Anyway, James Brown is in my CD-ROM, got ta get on the good foot

(secretly responsible for the mysterious circles appearing overnight in see British grain fields)*

you are the psychotic individual who placed the call, let us know and we'll send you a complimentary Circlemakers T-shirt! • you are considering marrying someone who has a history of cruelty and abusiveness; should you marry him since it is *possible* he might change? • you are unwilling to correct the inaccuracies – I think that is just fair • you are allowed to practice to ensure being observed, and you may enlist help, if only to ensure leaks, betrayals and vast further confusions • you are the reason progress continues • you are on your way • you are ashamed, feel guilty about having gulled people into claiming that your circle was made by diving supersonic pelicans, or were the result of emanations from car headlamps, lighthouses, or foaming pessaries • you are an "artist;" have been all along • you are proud, and show those bourgeois instincts which the *Guardian* will love, if no one else • you are an avant-garde landscape action-painter and just wanted to see the wonder of the theories your complex deceptions might give rise to • you are rendered mostly harmless again • you are at a distinct disadvantage • "you are not artists!" she is yelling to paroxysmal applause • "you are scum!" • you are talking about things that remain suspicious • you are now beginning to experience the double benefit of seeing almost false theories arise from possible falsehoods sponsored in turn by almost certain falsehoods • you are invited to start each day with Nancy Somers for an hour's yoga before breakfast • you are not concerned with such things • you are a criminal and will be severely punished • you are healing yourself with unconditional love • you are the reason progress continues to be made in these fields!

(not using the Force, Luke)

you are using alcoholic beverages and I really don't recommend emptying a whole glass each time • you are drinking if she's an Imperial, if something doesn't work on the Falcon (twice if it's the hyperdrive), if someone exclaims "No!," if someone does something apparently suicidal that turns out to be a good idea (twice if it's not Han), if Luke and Lando are in the same place at the same time (twice if they speak to each other), if Vader runs into one of his kids and doesn't recognize them (twice if he tries to kill them), if someone is mind-controlled using the Force, if Luke's parentage is foreshadowed, if people kiss (twice if they are closely related), if a Rebel pilot is of a race other than white (twice if they're nonhuman (co-pilots count); three times if an Imperial is of a race other than white) • you are so focused that the only thing you generally pick up is the atmosphere, the noise of the crowd, but very rarely is it anything specific • you are not likely to suddenly gain coordination from figure skating • you are the sculpture; quickness and strength are your tools • you are to be tense when working on a new or unfamiliar element • you are in the sport because you want to win an Olympic medal so not only are you going to fail, but you are going to waste a lot of time in the process • you are able to think about what to do, rather than how to do it • you are going to find it on absolutely every other page • dependent on hate you are for your attunement with the Force, but difficult it is to achieve attunement • you are returned without deposit • you are reckless, you stuck-up, half-witted, scruffy-looking Nerf-herder! • you are not a Jedi yet, but you are the only hope for the Alliance • you are using alcoholic beverages, I really don't recommend emptying a whole glass each time • you are drinking if someone wears the same outfit in all three movies (it counts if they change at the end)

(fucked up in your own special way)

you are fucked up beyond all recognition • you want to sound tough around new people so tell them that your nickname in high school was ol' mister dickhead • you are having a good time on the curb outside the 7-Eleven and that is perfectly all right • you are blind already (does too much jacking off make you see better or worse?) • you are under 13 • you are under 13, you sick son of a bitch • you are so pathetic • you are like "Mom, Dad, I love you (even though I don't)" • you are so fucking weak that I can't take it no more, everyone in high school is so fucking making fun of you • you are a disturbed child • you are sick for writing these perverted lyrics – get a fucking life • you are infected and you wonder if you will ever sit and read the dictionary again to follow the trails that lie beneath the words that query your lost innocence • you think you won't be worth a penny • you are songs that could never fully bestow meaning although it's been only two months since we first met • you are these feelings that I'm feeling deep inside • you are what I make of you • you are the true meaning of this phrase • you are what you make of it what you will it's your time to kill not mine because either way I am fine my life is still mine • you are saying you don't want to be in remorse? Well, whatever • you are the double life I'm leading • you are your own alpha and omega • you are the sum of someone else's ideas, values and actions • you are better off listening to some more competent musicians • you are wrong? Well, then: you are wrong and you'll suffer the consequences, young man, mark my words

(toiling, neither do you spin)

you are in the frame of mind where you are comfortable having
no history at all save a variable one • you are up to the task of
trawling through the inevitable flood of hopes and dreams that
will come your way • you are too busy to listen to this stuff • you
are getting sent? Oh, OK • you are taking the office tape pile out to
the wheelie bin tomorrow • you are in the over-40s crowd and
there is plenty of research to suggest that you are still having a very
active sex life • you are getting a Dell – I love those Dell computer
TV commercials featuring that kid • you are EarthLink, in which
event you sucked diligently 'til the end • you are still a piece of shit,
but I'm sure the people who developed you are kind souls who
meant well • you are a loser when you judge a seven-day period's
rate of excitement by the online journals you read • you are a
pathetic loser when you decide to act on that, in the form of incit-
ing violence • you are 11 • you are 11, we did it in 1992 and now
we've gone and done it again • you are, collectively speaking, 85
percent male and 15 percent female • you are Roman Catholic +2,
49 percent are Protestant -5 and 8 percent are "other" +2 • you are
big classical buffs, 73 percent • you are playing defence, complain-
ing that you have been misunderstood and issuing clarifications
• you are dealing with it, but you're out of order • you are out of
order • you are out of order

(your own secret twin preparing to make an appearance on *Ricki!*)†

you are underage or offended by such things so please stop reading now • you are now aware of what lies ahead, so if you read this and become offended, I take no responsibility, nor do I take any responsibility for children acquiring this story from less controlled sources, because I was 17 just a few years ago so I know what they can do • you are asking why? • you are interested, the shade is called: "Bimbo Blonde" • you are 30 and are definitely pushing it • you are pregnant with your fourth kid! But how are you going to make ends meet? With only two television shows you might have to pick up the slack and start co-hosting *The View* or something • you are a child of the '80s! Lindsay, I didn't say if you were born in the '80s • you are earning $20 mil + per movie; I think you can stand there and let the media take some photos of you • you are one sexy animal, you beast! • you are very nice • you are not driving home tonight • you are a fake and a fraud and you are gay! • you are in a boy band, or have even been in a boy band or have ever guest-starred on *The OC*, I'd love to meet you! Much love! xoxo • you are planning on sending her a note, please remember to use her new name • you are in trouble, who you gonna call? Oprah • you are who come here every day • you are too late! Yes, friends, I attended a Mary Timony show this evening with absolutely no catastrophes, nary a miniature Brad-localized rapture • you are not allowed to argue • you are going to need an eye patch • you are being spared • you are going to go out of your way to seduce young gentlemen, work your magic on someone who doesn't sound like a girl • you are in for a treat • you are the type of person who's going to miss *Providence*, you should probably begin making your travel plans to catch Celine Dion's new show at Caesars Palace in Las Vegas • you are a *Dawson's Creek* fan you probably already know Michelle Williams has a new movie, *Me Without You*, opening in select theatres this Friday • you are a first-time reader you probably would not have been able to guess that one • you are a tiny bit tired of hearing me saying that Bucks

County is a contender in the Hollywood game, so I will admit defeat this year • you are watching *Ellie*, you might be the only one • you are counting, that makes two • you are up for a road trip, the show's set for March 2 • you are probably thinking I spent the weekend booking a flight to LA • you are slated to be king, you can get away with cheesy lines like this • you are cynical and say it was only a romance in the mind of movie publicists and press agents • you are awed for a moment, then you go back to trashing the place • you are just not right when Neverland is the only place that feels like home • you are truly unlucky, crawling in and out of your private parts and trudging through pitch-black caves in bat dung up to your waist • you are convinced you can build a phaser out of your garage door opener and your camera's flash attachment • you are currently gathering the components to build your own nuclear reactor • you are a guy like Eames, nothing is taboo and not even your own brother's suicide is off limits • you are trying to figure out what's up with the opening scene where you see two men get shot in an African soccer stadium • you are dressing up as your toddler for Halloween • you are looking for something that suits the mood of the season without making your 13-year-old cry in fear • you are wondering why I don't put some of the more mainstream choices like the original *Star Wars* on here it's because I thought maybe they were a little too mainstream • you are correct • you are like me, you don't have TiVo, you don't have tons of money and you don't get a chance to watch a show week after week after week • you are like me, you don't get anything beyond bare-bones basic cable but I doubt you are that much like me • you are going to have some spare time and you are feeling really out of the loop • you are probably suffering from a bit of ennui • you are never in Los Angeles • you are willing to make a trip • you are hungry • you are so, so sick of the weather and longing for the hazy lazy days of summer, it is rare that we get an extended period of it here in this perpetually smiling landscape • you are forced to take the same routes over and over • you are half ++ +++++++++++++++++++++++++++++++ • you are going to see on TV this year: a forgotten and condemned man enjoying a foretaste of the freedom he believes will be his – someday • you are the guy who caught the guy who ate his victims • you are just out of luck • you are female, your name would be something like "Snælaug Björnsdottir" • you are gonna make a habit of crashing into innocent gargoyles • you are strong and tireless, frequently shouldering burdens that would tire lesser women • you are no "berserker" • you are a woman, they still think you are all right • you are interested in a factual understanding of the mysteries of life • you are not well-acquainted, you could feel quite alone and uncommunicative with new acquaintances or in a large crowd • you are the hippest, funniest, prettiest 28-year-old Shannon you can be • you are a robot to be reckoned with • you are gonna get seriously fired • you are all they have, lady • you are not falling into a literary rut • you are outnumbered, outflanked and out of options • you are infringing on copyrights owned by someone else • you are all that unique just because Jack and Jill went up a French hill and Leon and Starquashia went up a Brooklyn hill in a different novel • you are more than one person • you are one cool dude • you are a "star" that should have been receiving your self-righteous critique way before the 46 percent estimate fell down from the heavens • you are interested in becoming a writer • you are a black gay writer, you need to love black gay writers

(an immediately perceptible phenomenon elevated to the level of theological unity)

you are not endeavouring to extend your domain, nor have you need of territorial expansion • you are the most qualified and deserving of nations • you are, from every point of view, so happy, free from every worry and sadness – do you not worry for us? • you are living upon the great continent of the West enjoying the perfect liberty, security and peace of this just government • you are poor; you look within the treasure box but find nothing there • you are infidels and contaminated • you are living in a land of freedom • you are blessed with men of learning, men who are well versed in the comparative study of religions • you are situated, sometimes in your office, sometimes at home with your furniture and your food and cat, sometimes talking in the hall with the people in 14-B • you are an ignoramus; embrace it and defend it, for there is no praise too warm for you • you are the salt of the earth but failed to follow the principles presented above • you are under a curse and driven from the ground, which opened its mouth to receive your brother's blood from your hand • you are driving me from the land and I will be forever hidden from your presence; I will be a restless wanderer on the earth and whoever finds me will kill me • you are invited to register as many people as you wish • you are neither cold nor hot • you are wretched, pitiful, poor, blind and naked • you are busy with your own self instead of forgetting it and that your sense of unity is deficient • you are also in a position to assess how well-founded or ill-founded are the claims to knowledge of reality made by countless self-deceived prophets in the physical as well as the emotional world • you are right; all your brainwaves and imaginings agree with concensual reality • you are a perfected essential self and able to touch also the superessential world, even able to behold the solar systemic ruler in all his glory • you are by no means on "secure ground" merely because of that • you are omnipotent in the same worlds if you have a wee bit of reason left • you are such as the one you are condemning or will be such a one and will be condemned

• you are protected from self-deception • you are not liberated from emotional consciousness and its energies at once but only during a long series of incarnations, what is popularly called "ennoblement," with regrettably frequent relapses into the lower realms

(accurate to a depth of 30 m)

you are just getting started or you are an established user • you are
a winner because you know that Polar Bras tend to be tight and
you should try one size larger for a loose fit (you are also aware
that once a package is opened, it is not returnable) • you are not
sure • you are leaving • you are going • you are using again • you
are concerned with the seamless integration of hardware and
software • you are not training with others wearing heart-rate
monitors • you are on your way to success • you are looking for a
solid dot-matrix, a reliable laser, a multifunction printing device
or even a high-end colour printer • you are required to check your
air supply at regular intervals • you are OK at the end of a day • you
are responsible for cleaning up any mess and washing any salt
water out of the tray • you are one of them and we'll be happy to
honour your existing discount arrangements • you are vertical or
near-vertical when dumping air from vents at the top of the stab
jacket • you are too heavy but you head down and you're too light
• you are out of breath, E • you are a dead shark suspended in a
tank of formaldehyde but decomposing nonetheless • you are
diving from an unfamiliar hard boat or a rib, so make a pact with
another buddy pair that you will check with prior to moving off
the site • you are not using Samba for any reason • you are back in
black • you are just looking for a few answers • you are worried
about free flows so fill it slowly with very short, gentle blasts of
your octopus • you are sure they will be steady throughout • you
are swimming with the current and not against it

(pecs on your pecs)

you are training big, or do you flat out want to be big? Yeah, I thought so • you are already at the point where you can't brush your teeth because it hurts to lift your arms • you are working your pecs, you'll be strengthening your abs next • you are on a bench, let your arms drop to the sides and hang out to stretch your chest muscles • you are working hard to do a push-up • you are not working too fast or too slow • you are not stimulating them enough to make them stronger • you are a beginner, so use 5- to 10-pound weights while you learn the movement • you are already working with heavy weights, so be sure you perform all your reps with good form • you are working your pecs, you'll be strengthening your abs next • you are on a bench, let your arms drop to the sides and hang out to stretch your chest muscles • you are working hard to do a push-up • you are not working too fast or too slow • you are not stimulating them enough to make them stronger • you are a beginner, so use 5- to 10-pound weights while you learn the movement • you are already working with heavy weights, so be sure you perform all your reps with good form • you are using a stability ball, so sit on top of the ball, holding a dumbbell in each hand • you are going slowly enough • you are not stimulating them enough to make them stronger • you are not ready for the more difficult, classic push-ups • you are training chest, your target muscle is what? That's right, your chest • you are waiting for me to give you a full routine and tell you how many sets and reps to do, so get lost • you are placing the majority of the stress on the front delts • you are pumped to start today: "Bring on the bench press! Where are the car keys – I'm going to the gym!" Whoa, hold on there, Silver • you are blurring the line between maximal hypertrophy and muscle endurance • you are trying to peak for a max lift or break a plateau, but this probably isn't the best way to achieve steady improvements • you are jerked back to reality

(thrown out for lack of evidence)

you are Vittoria Romano, middle child and only daughter of the Dallas Godfather, Lorenzo Romano • you are the best suited to take over the family • you are recovering the files to use against Junior • you are the reigning princess of the crime family founded by your father, Lorenzo Romano, and you occupy a position of wealth and privilege • you are starting to wonder if it has more to do with rebelling against your father than any true emotional attachment • you are writing down a contact telephone number in case we need to get in touch • you are witnessing the end of freedom of speech in this country thanks to this far-reaching law • you are reading something now that soon will be illegal too • you are nicer than God, even if that's blasphemy! • you are shopping for lawyers • you are driving to work to do some overtime after dinner and a couple beers and someone on marijuana and a motorcycle hits you out of nowhere and they don't get up • you are going in for reckless homicide • you are lucky and you make good legal choices, so you might not like them • you are not so lucky or you are not so wise or – let's be honest here – you are not so well-behaved, so perhaps you will • you are brainstorming and writing your essay • you are studying the "primary" source or from other essays about the text "secondary" sources • you are quoting from a written text, but have you given an in-text citation after each quote to indicate the page from which the quote is taken? If your answer is "no," you should revise your essay before submitting it • you are quoting from the Internet • you are a terrible speller, so get someone else who isn't to proofread for you, or check uncertain words with a dictionary • you are going back there soon so maybe you wouldn't mind using your influence to make me postmaster at Smith's Corners • you are not so very large; I hardly think you are a quorum • you are pregnant • you are probably wondering why they haven't considered the effects of poverty on pregnant women's diets • you are receiving fair and equitable treatment under the law, so read on • you are not natural

• you are the wrong spirit in the wrong body • you are wholly male, with no trace of the Goddess in you and there's something horribly wrong and you are completely unbalanced • you are not getting the results you had hoped for, so it might help to let the school and parents know that you are willing to take the time to pursue the matter legally

(a nested loop)

you are nested inside a loop --> <cfset inloop = listfindno-caseancestorlist, 'cfloop'> <cfif inloop neq 0> I'm running in the context of a cfloop tag • you are nested inside a custom tag • you are there --> <cfoutput> I'm running in the context of a custom tag named #incustomtag# • you are lonely --> I'm not nested inside any custom tags • you are the second entry because the first entry in the context stack is the cfif tag at the top of this file --> <cfoutput> <p>I'm custom tag #listgetatancestorlist,2#</p> <! -- output all the contents of the stack a line at a time --> <cfloop index="loopcount" from="1" to=#listlenancestorlist#> ances-torlist entry #loopcount# n is #listgetatancestorlist,loop-count#
 </cfloop>
 </cfoutput> <! -- determine whether you are nested inside a loop - -> <cfset inloop = listfindnocaseancestorlist,'cfloop'> <cfif inloop neq 0> I'm running in the context of a cfloop tag • you are nested inside a custom tag • you are there --> <cfoutput> I'm running in the context of a custom tag named #incustomtag# • you are lonely --> I'm not nested inside any custom tags • you are given a polyno-mial: an*xn + S˘ + a1*x + a0 if exponentiation is not a primitive operation, what's the naïve complexity of polynomial evalua-tion? who was Horner and what is his rule? Brain teaser: how can you compute x8 in 3 multiplications? Now use this trick to esti-mate how hard it is to compute xn for any n • you are talking about a single user or a small group of users running against a relatively small database E • you are just slowing down the response time a little • you are only allowed to open the database with certain parameters • you are still telling the database to do a lot of unnec-essary work • you are doing it wrong • you are tapping into the database's inherent ability, essentially telling it your intentions and trusting the database designers to have enabled the database software to know what's the most efficient way to deliver the results • you are talking about a single user or a small group of users running against a relatively small database E • you are just slowing down the response time a little • you are only allowed to open the database with certain conditions • you are still telling the database to do a lot of unnecessary work • you are doing it wrong when you do • you are tapping into the database's inherent ability, essentially telling it your intentions and trusting the database designers to have enabled the database software to know what's the most efficient way to deliver the results • you are asking if you are correct, but it is a bad pattern and I think I have to break those largemethods to smallerregards relatedclasses b/c messages in this thread appeared to contain links to these classes

(getting sleepy)

you are getting veeeeeery sleepy • you are getting veeeeeery sleepy
• you are into the ring thing • you are out of pretzels too! Seriously,
research shows people will turn to fatty foods during both good
and bad times • you are a procrastinator • you are getting sleepy •
you are at it, check out the four "golden rules" for ensuring qual-
ity zzzzzs • you are only aware of the thought processes in your
conscious mind • you are awake and your conscious mind works
to evaluate a lot of these thoughts, make decisions and put certain
ideas into action • you are asleep, so the conscious mind gets out
of the way and your subconscious has free reign • you are still
aware of what's going on, but your conscious mind takes a back
seat to your subconscious mind • you are a certified hypnotist •
"you are going to find you might not miss so much," grouched
Oak • you are pretty • "you are doing all right!" Then he vanished,
leaving Peter with a warm feeling in his heart • you are only aware
of the thought processes in your conscious mind • you are awake
and your conscious mind works to evaluate a lot of these
thoughts, make decisions and put certain ideas into action • you
are asleep and the conscious mind gets out of the way and your
subconscious has free reign • you are still aware of what's really
going on, but your conscious mind takes a back seat to your
subconscious mind • you are fully conscious, but you tune out
most of the stimuli around you • you are surprised by something
– a monster leaping from the shadows, for example • you are
drinking a chocolate milkshake, you'll soon taste the milkshake
and feel it cooling your mouth and throat • you are afraid; you
may feel panicky • you are aware that it's all imaginary • you are
playing pretend on an intense level, as kids do • you are thinking
about what's up on the screen • you are also highly suggestible •
you are paranoid and you get a ten percent discount, in case you
are cheap • you are here: • you are always free to change the
hypnotic experience or wake up at will • you are going to die some
time so quit bitching about it • you are probably sleep-deprived,

which means you are getting less sleep than you need • you are sleep-deprived "if you are falling asleep at times when you don't plan to, that's a sign you are not getting enough sleep," says Thomas Roth, director of the Sleep Disorders and Research Center at Henry Ford Hospital in Detroit, Michigan • you are struggling to stay awake when inactive, such as while watching TV or reading; feeling tired when waking up; needing an alarm clock consistently to wake up; waking up often and having trouble going back to sleep; falling asleep after a heavy meal; having difficulty remembering or concentrating • you are reading this on the Internet, which suggests that statistically speaking, you are probably a post-adolescent male with a sticky keyboard and an embarrassing case of carpal tunnel syndrome; by all means we would like to continue to nurture this misconception so that we might convince you to place an order for the book right now

(an ode to the west wind)

you are wonderful, smart and witty; someone wants to spend the rest of her life making you happy (that someone is me) • you are rich enough to afford it • you ain't talking 'bout love • "You Are My Flower" – "Old Leather Britches" – "Across The Blueridge Mountains" – "Going Back To Harlan" – "Poor Rebel Soldier" – "No Hiding Place Down Here" – "Going Up Cripple Creek" – "Foggy Mountain Special" • you are also permitted, in fact, encouraged, to use the proceedings as a testing ground for paper topics and even for paper drafts • you are united • you are undivided • you are pure • you are brave • you are loyal • you are honourable • you are good • you are hopeful • you are true • You Are My Flower • you are interested in actuarial or computer consulting services • you are in their territories • you are used to looking at things in the world, not actions • you are on and ask what characteristics does this idea have? What else has those characteristics? Then watch ideas tumble out onto your page • you are using only one eye • you are Jessica Simpson, age 17

(made in your own image)*

you are famous • you are doing the 1963 thing, duh, you clearly want to be the hottest, chicest, sassiest girl from 1963, who still has really good hair and who once spent an April in Prague, living with a minor rock star • you are hilarious • you are fresh out of things to say about a men's gymrat tank top hanging loosely around a ratty lace underthing and a wan frame, with a big belt around the outside • you are just not sure what there is left to say • you are miserable, you are probably hooked on pills, and you have a deficient personality • you are supposed to wear something less slutty to traffic court • you are getting out of this one; Xenu asks that you recite to Leah Remini a thousand Hail Helatrobus oaths in order to make up for indulging in violence • you are the star of your own space opera, but that can be cancelled, if you get my meaning • you are in Great Britain, that means 21 minutes after the hour of 11 at night, and that is what time it is for Brooks Newmark, member of Parliament, first-time guest on *The Hugh Hewitt Show* • you are a long-distance runner, Brooks • you are brothers in the same office in some banal level • you are a new owner, you may buy a house and have the kitchen remodelled before moving in • you are the funniest man I no and the hottiest 2!!! sloane • you are awesome!! Hope you like this collage!! It's the background on my MySpace page • you are my hero! • you are one funny son of a bitch man! My friends and I quote you all the time!! "What!! I hope that it wasn't on my coat" Keep it up! Love the new CD! Peace! • you are the man • you are doing something worthy and artistic, then in the end, that can be a reward unto itself • you are just the people I was talking about • you are individuals who don't do these things to impress your friends! How many sites have you guys seen in which everything was just some inside joke depicted with a cat girl with anime eyes or someone trying to do something they want people to think they are • you are fooling yourself a little if you say "I don't care about the numbers at all!" Everybody who does this has a voice and wants to be heard • you

73

are closing the window, simply smile sincerely, wave, and if they can hear you say "See you tomorrow! Have a good one!" sincerely • you are willing to pony up the $2 • you are under oath • you are a terrible father, it said • you are dying to • you are being watched • you are shooting five hours after, you are not allowed to do it • you are going to contribute, now's the time • you are not doing anything wrong

(wanted)

you are the only one who can save the world • you are using a widget that won't let you experience the full wonder of the design and text formatting • you are not Mr. Creosote and there isn't a chance in hell you'll actually explode, but the thought is there • you are already a size 8 and working on an account where free Botox isn't uncommon, so it seems somewhat hypocritical when compared to the sudden urge to steal my chocolate • you are used to the ridicule • you are used to it • you are − > • you are shure 'nuff a redneck • you are both in the same grade • you are wearing a new outfit that you are feeling very confident in • you are noticed • you are energetic, ambitious and hard-working, so you can expect first-class rewards and real opportunities for international travel and career progression • you are free to live and work in the UK • you are an Elvis fan and you will probably find your way onto this CD-ROM

(a case of halitosis, gingivitis, dandruff and split ends)*

you are feeling • you are willing • you are supposed to • you are unable to detect any offensiveness; in fact, you detect "a pleasantness" • you are into it, and far more favourable rates than his New York City peers • you are always the one with the tight-lipped smile • you are impatient to find out, you have my symphonies

(a granny knot undone)

you are as competitive as you like • you are going to stain, so do it now • you are careful, use a lot of padding and take your time, you can get it back to almost perfectly straight • you are a member of the listserv, and should know that there are several topics on this • you are still overpowered, as described below by Daniel Feldman • you are too tight • you are too loose • you are in luck if you weigh 120 • you are below the line • you are over the line • you are pointing directly into the wind, look left – look right • you are but recently sainted • you are touched • you are always left behind? Never mind, Cinderella, kind Cinderella – [accenting each word with a twist of a strand of hair] nice good good kind good nice – Florinda [screams and slaps Cinderella]: not that tight! Cinderella: sorry • you are not coming • you are fearful of the woods at night • you are not to come and that is final • you are ignoring me • you are talking to your meal! • you are way up high and you look below at the world you've left and the things you know, little more than a glance is enough to show you just how small you are • you are way up high and you are on your own, in a world like none that you've ever known, where the sky's like lead and the earth's like stone, you're free to do whatever pleases you • you are really scared, being all alone and it's then that you miss all the things you've known and the world you've left and the little you own; the fun is done • you are back again, only different than before • you are everything maidens could wish for • you are climbing her hair and you see her up there, as you are nearing her, all the while hearing her "'a-a-a-a-a-a-ah" • you are ashamed of us • you are standing here stuck on the steps of the palace • you are not what he thinks that he wants? And then, what if you are what a prince would envision? Although how can you know whoyou are, 'til you know what you want, which you don't, so then which do you pick: where you are safe out of sight and your-self, but where everything's wrong, or where everything's right and you know that you'll never belong? And whichever you pick,

77

do it quick, 'cause you are starting to stick to the steps of the palace! • you are there, though, it's scary • you are still standing stuck on the stuff on the steps • you are so happy! Just as long as you stay happy, we'll stay happy! Cinderella • you are through and then into the woods you go again to take another journey • you are right • you are in the woods • you are clever • you are back to "or," which makes the "or" mean more than it did before • you are not bad, you're just nice • you are on your own • you are not alone • you are not alone • you are not alone • you are touched • you are always left behind? Never mind Cinderella • you are not to come and that is final • you are travelling so fleetly • you are ignoring some sensible advice • you are little Red Riding Hood and Mother said not to stray • you are a big tall terrible giant at the door, a big tall terrible lady giant sweeping the floor • you are back again, only different than before, after the sky • you are everything maidens could wish for! Cinderella's prince: Then why not? Rapunzel's prince: Do I know? Cinderella's prince: The girl must be mad! Rapunzel's prince: You know nothing of madness 'til you are climbing her hair and you see her up there as you are nearing her, all the while hearing her: ah-ah-ah-ah-ah-ah-ah-ah – both agony! Cinderella's prince: Misery! Rapunzel's prince: Woe! • you are not the man who started and much more open-hearted than I knew you to be • you are passionate, charming, considerate, clever – Baker: it takes one to begin, but then once you've begun, it takes two of you • you are ashamed • you are standing here stuck on the steps of the palace • you are through and then into the woods you go again to take another journey • you are right • you are in the woods • you are clever • you are back to "or," which makes the "or" mean more than it did before • you are not bad, you're just nice • you are on your own • you are not alone • you are not alone • you are not alone

(a piece of performance art that deep down inside wants to be a bust of Beethoven)

you are an asphalt athlete – yo, brave man – now give me a kick but if the sidewalk's cracked, you'd better pull out quick • you are the darling of my heart stay until the sun goes down shady grove, my little love shady grove • you are worried and upset about many things, but only one thing is needed • you are being faithful to the myth or that other sweet thing you are trying so hard to seduce • you are stammering that you are half blind, that you can read but not write • you are looking at ejaculate in trajectory • you are looking for something to completely soothe your stressed-out self • you are wearing a Superman cape • you are welcome in my office, he said • you are refusing protection and wandering about the city without a shred of defense • you are going to take it • you are not the grandson of a Russian immigrant • you are heading somewhere with this, Scully, but all of that is circumstantial • you are bleeding • you are on a roll • you are a protected witness • you are thinking with your bigger head again • you are playing on his level but the banjo player is drooling out of both sides of his mouth • you are a serious professional musician • "you are a great piano player but do you know you have a hairy ass and your balls are hanging out?" With a smile, the bum replied "Lady, know it? I wrote it!" • you are about to run him or her over with a steam-roller? Be flat, major • you are a banjo player and therefore need not be so hung up • you are booked to play the solo • you are cute • you are about to quit • you are there as a personal favour • you are singing in a language with which the conductor is the least bit unfamiliar, so ask her as many questions as possible about the meaning of individual words • you are going to stop, but you don't • you are going twice as fast as everybody else in the ensemble • you are being introduced as Bob Dylan • you are one ugly bastard! • you are seeking this amount of control with an orchestra? • you are Baba Muhammad • you are a stuffed shirt and listen to nothing but classical music and Debussy is your cousin • you are able to account for every moment and you have pinpoint awareness •

you are not terribly concerned about how people will perform your work 50 years from now, but given the difficulty of capturing your music on paper, would you want someone to come at your work through the score or your own recording? • you are dealing in a communicative gesture when you are making art • you are 54 years old and have certain needs which you are no longer able to satisfy • you are a fan of the man • you are out of cash • you are a hole behind me • you are still a hole behind, so you must be on the 13th hole • you are supposed to see – it's more of a feeling – an impression spoken in simple colour – orange, blue, surrounded by black

(a primal scream trying to differentiate yourself from an existential scream)

you are not dealing with your inner world • you are about to taste death and it will change you • you are here in my heart and my heart will go on and on • you are able with all your might to not necessarily produce a "deep" breath • you are a shallow breather, so try this simple test: put your palms against your lower abdomen and blow out all the air • you are on the right track • you are and do what you want, regardless of characteristic beliefs and actions • you are a jungle full of threats and predators • you are free from any domination or constraint to please self as self desires • you are calling the shots • you are the "terrible twos," rebellious youth, frontier mentalities, feudal kingdoms, James Bond villains, epic heroes, soldiers of fortune, "Papa" Picasso, wild rock stars, Attila the Hun, William Golding's *Lord of the Flies* and *Mighty Morphin' Power Rangers* • you are a kaleidoscope of natural hierarchies, systems and forms • you are the magnificence of existence valued over material production • you are Carl Sagan's astronomy, Peter Senge's organizations, Stephen Hawking's *A Brief History of Time* • you are gullible • you are not a plastic strip of advertising • you are just a little fish in the ocean of this computerized, electronic, space-age psychopathic ward and what use are my kisses if they only kiss the air? • you are being too obvious • you are lost in your Sputnik-NASA spacesuit and know that you'd rather be Dumbo the flying elephant but I'm sure that would be completely out of the question • you are if only you would listen to the sound of your heartbeat! • you are a song of dark love • you are blue song • you are dying, dying, dying a black horse on a white mountain, o scarlet girl, o the river of solitude, you cut my hands with your sharp blue diamonds, in my sleep breathe through me I'm your eyelids opening your tender heart • you are trying to waste their time; remember that your goal is not to win an argument but to provoke a futile one that runs forever • you are unaware that a bad attitude is our salvation! When they see their hair falling out they'll be sorry, but it will be too late! The slobbering masses are rats, are blank pages, are bacteria and they will burn when the last days come! • you are talking to idiots so treat them with the ill-respect they deserve • you are intense • you are much too sad don't be so tense some people said I don't belong how much ! long for a tender kiss it's you I miss it's you I think of every night I don't belong, I don't belong and still I fight to make it right and reach your tender heart • you are psychotic, when all I really want is your kiss! (January 5) • you are monkeys who beat off with their technological vibrators trying to prove that everything is nonsense except that one plus one equals two or somesuch other garbage • you are a direct result of a certain sensitivity in the bedroom but are just as shallow; logical positivists are boring people and they make excellent bankers and accountants because they like the things that are verifiable, because they like the things that make sense, for things like love and beauty are for Casanovas and womanizers and they make terrible womanizers, despising displays of passion and love play, they quantify and analyze every statement and see communication as a language game • you are Blessed! Yes, the herb of the gods is yours for the taking! The mutated natural winner (with no need of society) knows time control is his answer! The forbidden sciences teach that awareness protects our sacred abnormality which promises revenge on the black-suited killers who are a snare! • you are always quick to find fault in others, you watch your VCRs and your television sets, you drink your beer and your martinis, you drive your cars and see a lot of films of existential nature which you later discuss with your friends; you gentlemen always say how awful it all is, especially when you have too many drinks;, you gentlemen call it a weakness of yours and have another drink; you like to drink, you like to fuck and you like to watch television; you gentlemen appreciate beauty and finer things in life and that's why you drink, fuck and watch television; you gentlemen live for pleasure and excitement and you are a lot of fun at parties; you like to observe women's legs and asses and tits • you are wishing you only knew what you really think, that this is the best deal you will ever have but science cannot remove the terror of the gods! There is no hell deep enough for the doomed; their souls will be tasty treats for the near-omnipotent one! They will see their cities fall like children's blocks! They live only to work and die and you must unmask the false prophets who believe what they see on TV! • you are a fucker! But you probably know that already! Virgins are fuckers! Rednecks are fuckers! Married couples are fuckers! I love you, honey, but you are such a fucker! You fuckers take yourselves too seriously! You fuckers have no sense of humour! • you are the bullet! There is no coincidence! • you are no longer syntax • you are a poet • you are full of shit • you are tainted with the touch of the doomed! Their souls will be tasty treats for the fetid one, Cthulhu! They hear the divine jest and respond only with a blank stare! The evil deserve the witless law and order that they foist on us! We must not forgive them, because they know what they're doing and they will stare as dumbly as sheep when the saucers come • you are selfish and vain, don't write of your tears, you feel no pain, don't mention the big, you don't know the small, don't mention the small, it's boring to all • you are dead, she'll enjoy your dough and as for friends, they seem to come and go • you are or where you are going to • you are worth, for it's not worth a dollar to be a worm inside the earth – not a writer but a dullard! Oh yes! You even manage to get laid without wine or roses • you are restless and changing; show me • you are still my bleeding rose and neither hate nor death can divide our love my mind writes serenades for you like melodies of silence • you are a terrible angel descending down a spiralling staircase I welcome you are my saviour! What would I do without you?!" he says, running back to the apartment • you are in the milky moon O how tender is your walk through my eardrums I collapse in my drunkenness and watch the skies of wonder, I kiss

the thin fabric of your lips and journey through your hair I'm lost,
my love, in your negligee of white horses and silky winds • you are
full of shit • you are not a queer • you are bored and you scream:
"I want a new video, for this one I've seen!" • you are rich, if you
are poor • you are back now promoting the same old issues that
make me fall asleep • you are sick of it, expected to come up with
better shit – no, I'd rather be a local drunk and contemplate this
bar • you are saying? Just watch where you go, it's just a dead
possum that you squashed on the road • you are crazy or drunk,
it's a truck! • you are nothing – all you say, all you write, all you
hope for will amount to a big pile of nothing • you are new to
dreams and dreaming, so join us on dreamchatters • you are at
loose ends • you are more likely to be welcomed if you come with
gifts instead of garbage • you are in? Can you describe the old lady
in more detail and tell us any feelings you may have around her?
When you realize the rope is going to be cut, do you immediately
trust the decision or do you keep doubting that it will work and
fear for your safety? Can you describe the fireman/boyfriend in
more detail? Does he remind you of anyone from waking life? Any
feelings toward the girl feeding the shark? How about the shark
itself? • you are attracted to in more detail, characteristics that you
like • you are attracted to characteristics that you like, what he
reminds you of, etc. • you are in the building that I work in part-
time • you are welcome to make any comments you wish, what we
are teaching in this group is a non-defensive style developed by
John Herbert Montague Ullman Stage 11 variation modified for
e-mail • you are probably right • you are not always dreaming
about it and you can stay in touch with the reality of which trends
are which without sticking to only the crazy ones and having
everyone you love start to worry about you • you are in the right
place to hear them right now • you are ready to let him touch you
• you are ready for him • you are right • you are running from
something it's best to go lucid and turn right around while you

are in the dream and face the tornado • you are doing this in a dream, there's a big chance that there is no mental illness or chemical imbalance involved • you are headed down • you are at a time in your life where you need to make some decisions for yourself and your dad can't make it for you • you are going to leave home • you are in trouble however, stop! Go and talk to your dad, get some good advice and get back on track • you are holding onto him in your dream I would think this concerns your relationship and how you still feel about him • you are identifying with your masculinity • you are blaming the divorce on your dad and you might need to spend some time away from him until you can better deal with the divorce • you are being a little gullible when it comes to things that other people say to you • you are at a crossroads in your life and about to experience change • you are failing and the murders represent the goals or dreams in your life that are slowly dying or u think you can't accomplish? Hope it helps some • you are curious and unafraid and that you and your hubby remain alright and unharmed at the end of the dream, maybe mean that y'all will be alright no matter what changes y'all must go through, together or apart • you are scared of ending one chapter in your life falling off the cliff but are slowly realizing that the new chapter you are about to begin may be a chance for something new and beautiful symbolized by the baby as far as the handsome man falling with you, maybe you are looking for some one to talk to and to be with you through this change • you are asleep, as a way to relax and sort the days happenings out page 91 message: 513-025 [513-009] subject: re: balloons maybe the balloons represent your inner goals and things you want to accomplish in your life, the voice is merely you telling yourself not to worry and not to give up that some day you will "get the balloons" and make your "dreams" come true • you are thinking about your ex way too much and if the dreams bother you maybe you should find something to occupy yourself throughout the day so you are not mourning this break-up • you are the only one who can interpret your dream • you are alone • you are missing out • you are interested in contributing scanning equipment or software or other items, please contact Michael Hart • you are life, love, peace, truth and sanctity (a hockey stick broken over the spine of a 19th century hunch-back)*

you are wondering if this was way easier than trying to think of something original to say • you are trying to guess the meaning of composite or apparently composite words • you are run over by a steamroller negligent: a condition in which you absent-mindedly answer the door in your nightgown • you are one of the only things that can kill werewolves • you are very socially minded, constructive, and pretty hard to corrode • you are also pretty good about sticking up for yourself • you are shiny • you are "juggling" • you are friendly and well-liked, particularly for your sense of humour, although you sometimes play with people's heads • you are frequently the centre of attention and you like it that way • you are a Montrealer when please note, many of these apply specifically to Anglo Montrealers see point 4 you pronounce it "Muntreal" • you are secretly proud of their nerves of steel • you are not impressed with hardwood floors • you are a jazz afficionado • you are proud that Montreal is the home of Pierre Trudeau, Mordecai Richler, William Shatner, Leonard Cohen, Carmine Starnino and The Great Antonio • you are excellent with words and language • you are also good at remembering information and convincing someone of your point of view • you are making life very difficult for others • you are a plain ole cup of joe but don't think plain – instead think "uncomplicated" – you're a low-maintenance kind of girl • you are dependable too • you are a grammar god! If your mission in life is not already to preserve the English tongue, it should be • you are a great, wonderful, amaz-ing, fiancé/husband and are going to make a great father here soon • you are a child and once again you have demonstrated that you have no clue how to function in this world • you are two years younger than me and look ten years older, your husband's gut is as big as your ass, you are intellectually deprived and sexually frus-trated and your neighbors don't edge their yard but that gives you no right to torture me with the ingredients of your mother-in-law's turkey tetrazzini recipe or details about the dating habits of your husband's first wife • you are confident you can offer her a good time, and enjoy her company as well, but make it clear that you are comfortable admitting your shortcomings and quirks, too • you are reaping the consequences of your laziness • you are reading our title list • you are reading during Thanksgiving or Christmas break • you are in the throes of punctate pruritus? Trivia question #200: who would use a creel? Also featuring trivia on TV, music, kid, sports, history, movie, free, baseball, football trivia, basketball, trivia game quizzes, trivia, quiz, games, quizes, useless, facts, factoids, information, forum, fun, quiz, trivia quiz, science, triva, quizzes, quiz • you are allowed one free sample

(a healthy Hi-Pro glow)*

you are reading the manual for the setup instructions when you
come upon a rather astonishing page • you are funding, promoting
or endorsing the suppression of democracy and freedom whole-
sale and indiscriminate use of the death penalty commercial
harvesting of transplant organs of executed prisoners denial of
basic rights to Chinese workers and farmers nationwide forced
abortions and sterilizations sweeping and brutal repression of all
religions criminal psychiatric abuse of political prisoners routine
torture of prisoners military occupation and genocide in Tibet
draconian repression in east Turkestan military expansion and
aggression world's tightest Internet censorship and the largest
dealer of "weapons of mass destruction" to rogue states • you are
too lazy to read • you are Janet, that is • you are both? I've seen and
used good quality headphones with great sound, and it really
does make a difference • you are looking for that extra few mega-
hertz or just trying to save yourself from going insane over that
whining delta, water-cooling is definitely the answer • you are one
of the unfortunate thousands of people who have AOL as your
Internet service provider and you are extremely sick of hearing
that bastard say "Welcome, goodbye, you've got mail" every time
you want to use the Internet • you are looking for something
totally unique to cool your chipset and have about $34 • you are
looking for a more convenient, more compact look • you are new
but let's face it – square windows are boring • you are forming
your hairstyle • you are 50 or 60, plan now! If we have a war when
you are 18, enlist! Then once in, insist that they send you to the
front line or the most dangerous duty you can find! Or, let's say
you somehow fail to enlist • you are voted out the first week • you
are left with a series of jokes, asides, cliches and dumb bluster •
you are missing a leg or arm, you must insist it doesn't matter • you
are leaving! But they're pretty nice when they know you are harm-
less • you are behind this terrible curse, cease and desist, release
the Fijian people! They are sorry! Plus, that was 1867! He would've

died of something else anyway since then! And probably not have a really good story for his family to pass down! Who wants a boring story about Uncle Thomas serving as a missionary, coming home and dying of a heart attack at the age of 63? It's a little better to point to the shelf and say "There's the boots the buggers couldn't eat!" Past apologies have not helped • you are the President of the United States, you have a bag of tricks • you are deathly afraid of it just as it is, then it will fail faster because you've psyched them out! So I guess that makes me somewhere between being nice and Machiavellian • you are not entirely sure what's in it • you are running for class clown • you are just praying for your opponent to make a possibly boneheaded statement so you can pounce all over it, act disappointed in him, and score points for yourself • you are now in luck • you are king of the world • you are just a dog • you are so off my list

(Matisse's *Blue Nude* trying to get you to join the Jehovah's Witnesses)*

you are rotting from the inside • you are interested you are going to talk about God so learn respectful spelling and grammer please • you are an extremacist supremacist sect and your door-to-door is ineffective in spreading your message, so modernize • you are no part of the world, but I have chosen you out of the world, on this account – the world hates you • you are applying Bible principles in your home in order to produce a healthy and well-balanced environment in which to raise the child • you are a reasonable person by showing your flexibility and responding in an open and non-defensive manner • you are sensitive to the fact that your child may feel unusual, left out, or alienated by what may be a recent change in your religion • you are asked a question you do not understand or if you feel that the interviewer is getting at something other than what is stated, you should calmly ask the evaluator to restate or rephrase the question so that you may provide an accurate answer • you are able to communicate in an honest and natural way • you are the parent who will provide the better home for your child • you are the parent more capable of doing so • you are able to express this to the child • you are not opposed to medical treatment • you are capable and prepared to care for the child's physical needs • *You Are the Quarry* • *You Are the Quarry* released • *You Are the Quarry* released November • *You Are the Quarry* is out now in the UK and out December • *You Are the Quarry* 2-CD platinum edition set for October 18th release in UK • you are all fools! score: 0 to all of who are considering buying this deluxe edition but already have the original, let me tell you you are all idiots! And spare me from hearing any more "Paint A Vulgar Picture" lyrics from anyone trying to sound witty for the 359th time • you are all fools! by anonymous score: 0 Monday November 22 2004, @ 02:35 pm • you are all fools! by anonymous score: 0 Monday November 22 2004, @ 02:44 pm • you are all fools! by ghost of troubled jo score: 1 Tuesday November 23 2004, @ 08:50 am • you are all fools! by foolish_idealist score: 0

Tuesday November 23 2004, @ 12:31 pm • you are all fools! by wilde_oscar score: 1 Tuesday November 23 2004, @ 02:13 pm a simple, easy solution • you are a fan you would have "pre-loved" and kept looking brand-spanking new • you are all on the bread line • you are not to tell the police that? Jim Donald: no, not at all • you are going to be treated by the Church from now on? Simon Thomas: I don't know • you are repentant, you are allowed back into the congregation • you are not praying enough • you are anyway? Since when have you become the bee's knees on all of this? • you are presented with the association documents prior to signing a contract • you are excluding those who fall outside your parameters • you are advised prior to even signing your contract to purchase • you are wrong in their eyes • you are bored • you are and what you have done, what monstrosities have been done to you? Please – go away, you the exotic and too-human face • you are in the middle of the picture • you are working on a comprehensive video documentation of this theme! • you are referring to Schönberg's piece, specifically its recording by Nam June Paik, who let the record run at a quarter of its normal speed, and then its recording by Dieter Roth, who restored Schönberg's music to its original tempo by speeding up Paik's version • you are happy • you are getting warm • you are munching on a Nathan's, or, in my case, disputing the nutritional value of chorizo with the missus, you have the Moor to thank • you are getting into negative numbers there • you are directly addressing the right address even if your message involves stern criticism and disturbing frankness • you are the greatest critic of this mess even though you are accused of also being its greatest supporter! • you are right, my image of a hacker has in fact a lot to do with such an image of the artist • you are the designer, you define the rules, but then you get involved and become part of the game yourself, and the time has come to quit

(the distance between the hyperboic curve at the y-axis)*

you are an open-minded individual that thinks for yourself or is your knowledge the result of a Google search or quoting established scientists? Please give me a chance to change our understanding of the nature of our universe, or if you prefer, correct the errors in my logic • you are implying that no one can learn anything from established scientists or Google searches • you are the only one who does have a grasp of the situation? And you expect to be taken seriously after espousing such a position? • you are mistaken and you have not given a sufficiently detailed explanation for that argument • you are still playing with your chimney; I had the same problem • you are getting way off the topic and sounding like a loony • you are definitely a loony • you are a loony • you are trying to say something, could you ellabirate on your answer • you are promoting flawed ideas and spreading false assertions • you are looking over huge distances • you are straining the credibility of your thesis • you are wasting our time • you are wrong • you are misunderstanding the analogy • you are arguing here • you are missing the point • you are absolutely right regarding the ability to test the hypothesis locally • you are right, "we," i.e., the "main-stream," are making huge errors • you are restricted to the intervals used therein • you are really determined to print it anyway • you are encouraged to cooperate with each other in working on anything in the course, but what you put in your journal should be you • you are inside • you are either born with it or you are not • you are right • you are welcome to discuss this issue on some other Wikipedia page, but please leave this page alone

(what you eat)

you are into it as long as it's passionate – a man has a shelf life of
at least five years • you are quite touched by it, you think it's nice
of him but you can't help but wonder what his "problem is" – you
imagine yourself as: a queen or an empress an actress a writer a
business leader golden girl • you are involved – when he gives you
the silent treatment • you are in the middle of "it" • you are willing
to give it a shot so you jump his bones instead – the next time you
eat out

(a reified universal transcendental signifier)

you are sliding along another axis somewhere • you are wildly fourspacing it • "you are all text," jennifer says – >
<! – "there's nothing to me," agreeable alan – >
<p><form> <input type="button" name="b1" value="spread me" onclick= "alert 'you spread my arms and legs';"><input type="button" name="b1" value="open me" onclick="alert 'you spread me on your screen';"><input type="button" name="b1" value="splay me" onclick="alert 'your trembling hands';"><a name="dd"> </a><input type="button" name="b1" value="cut me" onclick= "alert 'you spread me on your screen';"><input type="button" name="b1" value="fuck me" onclick="alert 'you spread me on your screen';"><input type="button" name="b1" value="sing to me" onclick="alert 'your fingers down my throat';"><input type="button" name="b1" value="suck me" onclick="alert 'you pull you out of me';"><input type="button" name="b1" value="hold me" onclick="alert 'your palms on me';"><b> <tt><font color="#ffffff"><font size=+1>murmur you aren't more, alan</font></font></tt><font size=-1>turn me into <a href="exp • 'you are taking me';"><input type="button" name= "b1" value="call me" onclick="alert 'you spread me on your screen';"><a name="ee"></a><input type="button" name= "b1" value="be me" onclick="alert 'you spread me on your screen';"><input type="button" name="b1" value="kiss me" onclick="alert 'my body is yours';">churn me into<a href="exp • 'you are tearing into me';"><input type="button" name="b1" value="yearn for me" onclick="alert 'soiled hole';"><input type="button" name= "b1" value="pine for me" onclick="alert 'bruised nipples';"> <input type="button" name="b1" value= "piss for me" onclick= "alert 'you are staining me';"><input type="button" name="b1" value="come to me" onclick="alert 'you spread me on your screen';">against my<a href="exp • "you are all text," jennifer says – >
 another experiment in wryting the html body

(kind of pissed off that you were never given the choice of whether to be a sequitur or not)

you are missing out • you are overdressed • "you are not my type," her eyes seemed to say • you are growing up • you are missing out on the good stuff • you are interested • you are the only person in line • you are on the rag • you are horny so it's lust, but if your partner's horny, it's affection • you are surrounded by turkeys • you are always at it • you are sorry every five minutes • you are having flies • you are serving it up • you are famished • you are the bird and sometimes you are the windshield • you are in it up to your ears, keep your mouth shut • you are missing out • you are overdressed • you are growing up • you are going 5-10 mph less than 79 mph, you are a safety hazard to not only yourself, but to others on the road • you are signing, but it's too late to complain when you've burned your fingers • you are tricked • you are not happy with the terms and you can find another fairly easily, if you read it and give them your business and break the rules and bitch about it you are really asking for it • you are driving down the road at about 10 mph over the speed limit, then suddenly I whiz by you going much faster • you are way off by Ender Ryan, 06/25/2001 09:07:19 am EST • you are always free and safe to express yourself though you may not be spared thoughtful challenge • you are referencing the momentum of criteria specifically, but is there no "choice" happening? I grasp the movement of "choiceless awareness," yet grapple with the sense that vigilance is a choice I seem to be making • you are a published writer • you are speeding, then we have a privacy issue, but not when you are renting other people's property • you are or were sick of this song, you are free not to read on

(and if you aren't who is)

you are over 18 • you are younger than 60, you won't take a supply
of Finnish meat balls and sausages with you • you are male or over
40 or under 12, you maybe drink milk at every meal • you are over
15 or, in some circles, over 10, or over 8 and under 65, you have a
cellular phone and you use it, all the time • you are over 35, you
and your friends tell each other horror stories about how miser-
ably few facts of history and culture modern kids really learn at
school while in "Europe," as you know, children are still forced to
memorize important names and dates and read several national
classics • you are older than 50, you might remember a time when
well-off people could take a ferry to Stockholm to buy things one
couldn't get at home • you are under 45, you are more or less
familiar with Lucky Luke, Tintin and Asterix but not Moebius –
and, of course, the Simpsons • you are over 65, you learned at
school that Germany is the leading nation in Europe and
European culture and helps us against the eastern Barbary • you
are younger, your attitude towards Germany may be a little
ambivalent, as you have consumed a lot of Anglo-Saxon films,
books and comics about World War II • you are a young urban
male, 18-25, perhaps even the strange American version of so-
called "football" • you are most probably a Lutheran over the age
of 30, which usually means that you go to church at Christmas or
never, get married in church and have your children baptized •
you are usually a 20-year-old of foreign descent or an intellectu-
ally oriented convert looking for "something different" • you are
25-35, accustomed with the state church and religion, maybe
even God being there but don't want it them to interfere with
your life • you are middle-aged (30-40) or younger and urban,
you believe in a kind of all-European gourmet cooking anything
from pesto to paella and also visit McDonald's or other junk food
places • you are old (over 60) and rural, you eat rye bread and
potatoes every day, with either fish mostly Baltic herring in
different forms or "sauces" with different kinds of meat • you are

not really a racist but at 25, still unaccustomed to different races, maybe a little xenophobic • you are a male and under 30, you might get aggressive if you see black-haired or dark-skinned foreigners in the company of Finnish women • you are taught at school until you are 18 • you are a female younger than 25, you want a romantic church wedding if you are a member of the church, no other ceremony by "worldly" authorities is required • you are middle-aged (40) or older, you believe that most Swedish men are gay • you are a woman under 40, you perhaps occasionally go to the beach topless depending on which beach • you are not going to die of cholera or other third-world diseases because you are under 30 • you are a young patriot and are extremely annoyed when foreigners take famous Finns, cellular phones or saunas for "Swedish" • you are a teenage female walking alone • you are finished before you started

(not enough to get over the threshold)

you are gutsy, you can try to strafe your opponent, easily smearing him with torps and hoping he doesn't react fast enough to take you down too: this often ends in a fiery mutual annihilation • you are doing about 25 points or more, less damage isn't really worth it • you are quite capable of circling a planet cloaked again and again while the enemy pours fuel into empty space • you are good – you can hold against several cautious enemies, or several over-enthusiastic ones • you are increasingly unable to maintain an accurate perspective as to how well you know it • you are good at hustling product from the back of the room • you are history • you are already an expert at platform mechanics • you are on the threshold of going out on your own, fresh challenge surface • you are not yet ready, willing and able to invest in my personal services • you are ready to rocket your speaking career to the next level, I'm here for you! Make the most of this cyber-adventure! My wish for you is that you create all the speaking business success you want for yourself and your loved ones • you are doing well on meds, but have some higher risk exposure to someone who has a strain of HIV that is resistant to your meds – it is possible that this new HIV could take hold • you are the one who has to live with your armour, let it suit your needs • you are ready to make your first insertion • you are putting pins under your skin, you must do so with tacit knowledge of the pain and suffering that your forebears had to go through • you are preparing • you are to insert pins all around your leg you are liable to sever your skin • you are actually a planet taker until it's too late

(getting even sleepier)

"you are becoming more focused on certainly more pleasurable thoughts and that sense of comfort is relaxing, isn't it?" If you noticed some grammatical inconsistencies in that last sentence, you have already begun to notice one of the characteristic hallmarks of Ericksonian technique • you are under arrest for spying and you are coming with us • you are a British spy from London, England • you are a threat to us, with you being the enemy and all, so perhaps I can change your way of thinking • you are struggling so hard to keep them open • you are only paying attention to my voice and nothing else • you are overweight but we have become more and more aware of how common the disorder may be in slim patients • you are sick – when you have a cold, flu, infection or other illness • you are sick, you should take the following steps immediately: tell your doctor that you are sick • you are taking diabetes pills, you may have to switch to insulin instead • you are sick • you are sick • you are sick • you are losing weight • you are sick – when you have a cold, flu, infection or other illness • you are sick, you should take the following steps immediately: tell your doctor that you are sick • you are taking diabetes pills, you may have to switch to insulin instead • you are sick • you are sick • you are sick • you are losing weight • you are under my power • you are feeling relaxed • you are relaxed • you are now perched on your nest, my little bird • you are in my power • you are sick • you are sick • you are right • "you are going to make ..." he explained, as both girls listened intently, "... you are excited to record your first album," he said

(a fine piece of work)*

you are on the right side of the law? • you are breaking the law •
you are caught red-handed, you'll likely get sued, not charged
with a crime • you are good, we give you money, if you are a dick,
you are faded • you are not allowed to see what it looks like • you
are disturbed by the misleading "Midwest Heroes" ads • you are
one of them • you are giving – tomorrow • you are the one play-
ing the Fifth Symphony on your pennywhistle, you'd better
contact the orchestra before dropping a piece into your electronic
suitcase • you are training two or three people in a cubicle and
playing a CD as background music, no license is needed, Bell says
• you are being watched • you are a pirate • you are not interested
in purchasing bells and whistles at this time since bells and whis-
tles do not impress you in the least • you are being a little gener-
ous to Sony toward the end there • you are purchasing a music CD
with similar DRM software on it, you'll never open the package,
instead downloading the mp3 files for that album through illegal
P2P file sharing • you are feeling demanding or just want to toss
a comment her way • you are a child and must go home and have
a nice cup of cocoa

(a stupid English knight)

you are here: • you are part of the future • you are Beatles with an "a" • you are really a gem • you are still a rat • you are Japan • you are an ass • you are interested in sending a phobia name to me, please send the reference for it • you are under 21 years of age, immature, a legal scumbag, a shallow journalist, a P • you are scaring me! I'm not talking to myself • you are not • you are talking alone • you are right • you are storing the graphic • you are bored – 258 things to do when you are bored – wax the ceiling • you are really bored • "you are this young one's protector also?" Odin: "It seems that way" • you are my new master • you are it • you are naïve • you are it • you are visitor number 336 to this page • you are an idiot so open it and remove all doubt

(search and destroy mode)

you are on system and you have my sympathies; you are now on your own • you are in luck • you are ready to test the code • you are on foot, trudging the enemy occupied island in search of the CK 23 orbital interceptor – a piece of kit capable of shuttling from the atmosphere into space then dropping back to knock out enemy missiles • you are in your direction of travel • you are now controlling a gunsight • you are inside you may just find empty shelves, but there could also be more ammunition, explosives or batteries for your mine detector • you are accustomed to it, but eventually you'll sort it out • you are requesting authentication and not file locking • you are connecting, even if you link with no compatibility • you are not the intended recipient please notify Hale and Dorr immediately by telephone or by e-mail • you are in the bin directory, type: • you are in any other directory, type: • you are real quick, you'll see this message before entering: • you are almost ready to go see the next section • you are finished, double-check for typos, then press ESC

(a 60-cycle hum)

you are wrong • you are right because someone else is wrong • you
are always on your own • you are still afraid of me • you are all
alone • you are all alone again • you are still alone • you are in a
class all alone • you are the leader and they follow like sheep, they
are and what, yeah, keep on believing you • you are not • you are
listening anymore • you are punk so you rebel against the scene

(a refutation of the Special Theory of Relativity)

you are justified in declaring that model as false! This brings us to the next myth: modelling myth #6: • you are a deftly turned phrase, an etymological landscape, a home by the sea • you are the message on a cassette tape long after it has been recorded over • you are a festering wound incurred in a skirmish in the war between the u • you are used and abused • you are a distress property bought by Tom Vu and sold for an outrageous profit • you are ossifying sweat on Robert Plant's perfor- mance towel, now in the possession of a man who is thinking about auctioning it off because he has decided he would rather listen to "new country" • you are an onion ring with an identity crisis on the Korona Restaurant's "Transylvanian Meat Platter" • you are an easy-riding H that just knew you would be stopped by police, cuffed, hauled in and strip searched while you were making your way through the mountains in Georgia • you are everything your mother had hoped for, and more • you are track lighting gone bad, a one-time energy saver now driving a gas-guzzling '71 Impala • you are considering touching that dial • you are a pretense to uni-versality • you are the top quark • you are one of a family of Dirt Devil carpet cleaners • you are wondering at this moment whether you are merely a cleverly disguised rip-off • you are a foreign agent who accidentally ruptured an emer- gency cyanide tooth cap just before your rendezvous with a thin man in a lumber jacket standing by a garbage can on the patio of a McDonald's in Paris, who was to receive an attaché case containing vital information photo-reduced on microfilm which, of course, you have no prior knowledge of • you are a mispronounced word with eyes stuck in an awkward position just like your parents warned you they would, trying to get a date with one of the "cool chicks" in your high school and hav- ing a difficult time of it • you are fibre ingested by a septuagenarian to promote regularity • you are a face in the crowd • you are secretly responsible for both the mysterious circles appearing overnight in British grain fields and getting the soft- flowing caramel into the Caramilk bars • you are not using the force, Luke • you are fucked up in your own special way • you are toiling, neither do you spin • you are your own secret twin preparing to make an appearance on *Ricki!* • you are accurate to a depth of 30m • you are pecs on your pecs • you are a nested loop • you are getting sleepy • you are an ode to the west wind • you are made in your own image • you are a case of halitosis, gingivitis, dandruff and split ends all rolled up into one • you are a granny knot undone by an older and wiser scout leader • you are a piece of performance art that deep down inside wants to be a bust of Beethoven sitting on a Steinway grand piano • you are a primal scream try- ing to differentiate yourself from an existential scream • you are a hockey stick broken over the spine of a 19th century hunchback you figured had no business playing street hockey in the first place • you are a healthy Hi-Pro glow • you are what you eat • you are a reified universal transcendental signifier • you are kind of pissed off that you were never given the choice of whether to be a sequitur or not • you are not enough to get over the threshold • you are get- ting even sleepier • you are a fine piece of work, you are • you are a stupid English kon-igght • you are currently in search and destroy mode • you are a 60-cycle hum • you are a refutation of the special theory of relativity • you are a parade of endless details • you are the lusts of your father • you are wondering at the audacity of some people who like to tell you just who they think you are • you are a means of production • you are the line cut out of the final edit by some guy using a PowerBook in a cheesy local laundromat, or if you aren't you wish you were • you are being com – 52 *Object* Wershler-Henry and Kennedy page 5 – pletely irrational • you are the wrong answer on the multiple choice section of the LSAT • you are feeling quite overwhelmed, you must say • you are exactly what they've been looking for and that should frighten you • you are the significant answer in an inkblot test • you are well on your way • you are the space between the heavens and the corner of some foreign field • you are rendered completely useless • you are a B- grade on a C paper • you are so beautiful to me • you are a game of tic-tac-toe that, after dealing with an inferiority complex, beat up a game of "glob-althermonu- clearwar" and kicked the shit out of Pentagon computers • you are on your way to the store to get a litre of milk, when this cow with the head and antlers of a moose sporting a black eye patch over his left eye comes up to you and says "you are on your way to the store to get a litre of milk, when this cow with the head and antlers of a moose sporting black eye patch over his left eye comes up to you and says 'you are • you are the weak argu- ment in an elaborate doctoral thesis • you are the mira- cle cure for halitosis, gingivitis, dandruff and split ends all rolled up into one, at least that's what your 19th century procurer • you are not but let's say you are • you are your favourite letter of the alphabet except h cuz that has already been taken • you are an ass- hole ee- o-ee-ole • you are a soliloquy on a barren heath in a play which inspired Shakespeare's *King Lear* but has been lost for many centuries, last documented in the Earl of Derby's private collec- tion in 1723 • you are billed as the "nicotine patch to the world" • you are everything you want in a drugstore • you are only as good as the next guy • you are the eggman, you are the eggman, you are the wal- rus goo goo a' joob • you are shovelling shit in a Roman stable • you are dead now, so shut up! • you are in the process of being palimpsested • you are an inces- tuous mess • you are available only through this limited TV offer • you are the party of the first part • you are a no-good, lazy son of a bitch • you are often replaced by an • you are a big waste of time, for the most part • you are surely mistaken • you are a detachable penis • you are therefore you think • you are the side effects of performance-enhancing drugs • you are a bad case of blue-balls • you are boldly going where no man has gone before, but only as the disposable crew member who happens to be dumb enough to talk to a lump of painted grey Styrofoam and therefore, in my humble opinion, deserves to get it any- way • you are translated into 20 different languages • you are not smart, just hard working • you are a painting bought solely for the frame • you are the one really likes it, really • you are not a machine, you are a human being • you are corn, but we call it maize • you are dumb enough to spend your time typing out endless statements that begin with "you are" just to make a point and try to get some laughs, neither of which, in retrospect, you believe you will succeed in • you are the interest accrued overnight by some clever electronic banking maneuver • you are misspelled in a grade six spelling bee by a kid who will eventually serve eight years in jail for manslaughter • you are better than bad, you are good • you are a quote within a quote desperately trying to escape • you are a most noble swain • you are in absentia • you are engaging in self-nullifying behaviour • you are a vague sense of alienation masked by a friendly, conversational atmosphere • you are a dentist, you take delight in causing great pain • you are the kind of apathy that can only be generated by the "spoken-" vs • you are a self-consum – 53 *Object* Wershler-Henry and Kennedy page 6 – ing artifact • you are an unimportant stanza in an unimportant Bob Southey epic • you are the neuro-chemical dopamine bridging the gap between the tail of one synapse and the head of another during a bout of particularly raunchy sex with a not-quite-loved one • you are an instance of pre-emptory teleology • you are living in a post-theory, post-language writing, post-sound-poetry, post-literate age, so let's stop writing crap that pretends that you aren't • you are a reference to the small font size of this poem • you are going to sell out the first chance you get • you are yawning – stop it! • you are a persnickety line removed at the friendly request of an editor who thinks its potential offensiveness is enhanced by the mere fact of its referential obscurity • you are all out to get me, damn you! • you are sitting with a soggy ass at some reading in High Park really wishing you were somewhere else • you are a portable Greek reader that is going to party like it's 1999 • you are going on with your doggy life • you are the interplay between the quotidian and the extraordinary • you are a rav- enous, meat-eating carnivore who lusts after the feeling of animal blood tracing the crevasses of your chin, or if you aren't, you know one • you are a captain's log, sup- plemental • you are a metonymic slide • you are a pipefitter with a penchant for Descartian ontology • you are everyday people • you are believing this crap they're feeding you • you are convinced you looked better before the makeover • you are a bird, no, wait, you are a plane, no, hell! you are Superman! • you are an uninterrupted series of dots that hasn't come to terms with being a line yet • you are a linguistic trap set to catch some good eatin' possum • you are eleven benevolent elephants • you are a regis- tered trademark of the Coca-Cola Corporation • you are the supreme arbiter and lawgiver of music • you are woman, hear you roar • you are never going to amount to a hill of beans in the world • you are bad advice foisted on some lovesick puppy • you are an axiom proved false • you are the cruellest month • you are flown to your destination on Delta Air Lines • you are the book in the spir- it machine • you are a Dadaist who needs to love and be loved • you are hoping that you will never have to hear that fucker read his damn "you are" poem again but are resigned to that fact that you probably will • you are in more closets than you wish to admit • you are someone with the debilitating habit of cutting against the grain • you are going, going, gone • you are a likely consumer of rubber nipples • you are a long-lost jazz score that no one would have played anyway • you are a last will and testament • you are an unceremonious exit the preceding analog version of "apostrophe" was written by Bill Kennedy ca. • you are new to science • you are getting more than you expected

(a parade of endless details)

you are doing your walk, don't just walk by the window a few feet away and casually glance at it, do what the burglars/perverts do • you are an inch from the opening • you are interested in using any portion of her work please contact her directly • you are bombarded with ELFs every day • you are doing and pay attention, whether it's a radio spot, billboard, a TV commercial, or a magazine ad? Chances are, the messages that do the best job of attracting your attention are the ones that focus on how a product or service will make you feel better, provide you with comfort, pleasure, solve a problem, infuse your marriage with romance, attract the opposite sex, bring your family closer together, make your life easier, healthier, safer, more secure, prosperous, exciting or more fun • you are among the successful minority! You are ready to check out simply type in "birthday" as your coupon number on the first shopping cart page and then click the "Enter" button • you are in business to make money and we are here to further that goal by giving you the best tools in the world • you are persuaded by the editor's opinions of power in the pages of today's computer and Internet magazines, you may eventually be disappointed • you are not pre-registered • you are really feeling energetic, you may want to sign up for the Chinese New Year YMCA 10 km/5 km/run/walk, which starts at 8 am on Sun • you are going to have a star of Yeoh's calibre in your action film, why not use her abilities appropriately? *Tomorrow Never Dies* does have a few nifty but average spy gadgets • "you are my sunshine!" (your price: $39) • you are interested in one of the items but it appears to be out of stock, please bookmark this page and try again later

(the lusts of your father)

you are invited to a free *Bar-B-Q* it will only cost you your soul
• you are thinking? Do you have to get drunk in order to save a
drunkard? Or: • you are playing with fire and will get burned? •
you are approving of their sins by participating and being a bad
example • you are different, you've got something "special" • you
are young, the challenges life may bring seem to be exciting, for
one thing: you'll meet new people and go places • you are running
short on time and phrases • you are older, you'll take a different
view of the fun you did have and foolishness you did do • you are
a majority in any situation • you are not your own? For you were
bought at a price; therefore glorify God in your body [and in your
spirit], which are God's • you are now in comparison to where you
were: without Christ, a slave of sin, without hope • you are doing
is great, but you possibly should be a little more open-minded •
you are judging too much • you are closed-minded and you will
never be as good a Christian as I am • you are now a child of God
and a member of the family of God • you are now a member of
God's family, don't let anyone tell you different • you are not good
enough • you are made up of spirit, soul and body • you are born
again, in Christ Jesus • you are mindful of Him and the Son of
Man that you visit Him? For you have made him a little lower
than the angels and you have crowned him with glory and
honour • you are in for a big surprise

(wondering at the audacity of some people who like to tell you just think)

you are neat I think your life is incomplete but maybe that's not for me to say they only pay me here to play I wanna hear a caravan with a drum solo you're probably wondering why I'm here and so am I so am I just as much as you wonder 'bout me staring back at you yeah! That's just how much I question the corny things you do you paint your face and then you chase to meet the gang, where the action is stomp all night and drink your fizz roll your car and say gee whiz you tore a big hole in your convertible top what will you tell your mom and pop, I tore a hole in the convertible you're probably wondering why I'm here and so am I so am I just as much as you wonder if I mean just what I say that's just how much I question the social games you play you told your mom you stoked on town and went for a frooze in Freddy's car Tommy's asking where you are you boogied all night in a cheesy bar plastic boots and plastic head and now you think you know where it's at you're probably wondering why I'm here not that it makes a heck of a lot of difference to you but watch George • you are so fine? But I wouldn't throw away the groovy life I lead 'cause baby what you've got, yeah it sure ain't what I need girl you'd better go girl you'd better go away I think that life with you would be just not quite the thing for me why is it so hard to see my way? Why should I be stuck with you it's just not what I want to do why should an embrace or two make me such a part of you I ain't got no heart to give away-ay-ay ain't got no heart ain't got no heart ain't got no heart ain't got no heart to give away • you are so neat I don't even care if you shave your legs wowie zowie, baby you are so fine wowie zowie, baby please be mine wowie zowie, up and down my spine I don't even care if you brush your teeth I dream of you each morning I dream of you each night just the other day I got so shook up I dream of you in the afternoon baum didi baum didi baum didi baum didi baum didi baum didi bam bam bam bam bam • you are pondering my redundancy – nobody wants to hear about all of this end of civilization stuff anymore • you are wondering, that's the "awful" line that normal underwear causes in pants • you are now good with God • you are so nice – or alternatively it might be someone who is angry and complaining • "you are all screwed dudes! Ha ha ha!," as I taunted them in my fresh and clean Bobby Brady plaid pants • you are as righteous as I was • you are free to print out this article for your personal use

(lost in the aphasic shuffle)*

you are like most people • you are perfectly rational • you are puzzled by what you see • you are welcome to print out this book for distribution to anyone that you think would be helped by reading it

(means of production)

you are a multiple-choice survey • you are situated, sometimes in your office, sometimes at home with your furniture and your food and cat, sometimes talking in the hall with the people in 14-B • you are increasing your milk supply • you are producing and delivering because breasts don't come with any measuring devices • you are now 3-4 months postpartum, you are at the point where milk secretion becomes completely autocrine controlled • you are trying to increase your milk • you will need to dip into that 20 percent residual using extra nursings with baby and extra pumping when you are away • you are going to the core office to fill out the appropriate forms • you are not familiar with the current program in expository writing and would like further information before applying for a position so you are visiting the expository writing office • you know that should apply at the registrar's examinations office but are too lazy • you are cyborg • you are cyborg by Hari Kunzru for Donna Haraway and we are already assimilated • you are a collection of networks, constantly feeding information back and forth across the line to the millions of networks that make up your "world" • you are very likely to get notions of tape loops, communication breakdown, noise and signal – amazing stuff • you are a rice plant • you are a researcher trying to wean the Californian farmer off pesticides • you are going to have to pitch it to someone – a producer, a director, a production executive, an agent or anyone in the business • you are pitching a story and while character and action may be the glue that holds everything together, it all starts within the context of story • you are setting up the story and need to know who the story's about including the changes that he or she goes through; in other words, what it is about your story that will make an audience plunk down the cost of admission for your movie • you are pitching someone who is hanging on your every word • you are wearing your best shoes which goes into the whole package of what makes a good pitch • you are going to sell something to me that you are not committed to, no matter what, because I can smell it • you are driving to work to do some overtime after dinner and a couple beers and someone on marijuana and a motorcycle hits you out of nowhere and they don't get up • you are part of a group actively trying to subvert the constitution, destroy morals and pay more democrats to get into political office • you are nothing more than an agreeable part of the enemy • you are hoping to start a business relationship • you are in it up to your eyeballs now • you are desperately cheering on your nearest and dearest or simply going along to soak up the carnival atmosphere • you are at the top of Canary Wharf, in which case you can watch the runners make their way from Tower Bridge through Shadwell and Limehouse from 800 ft above the course • you are watching your co-workers • you are happy to receive this contact from the BBC so please tick here • you are looking for a particular artist, composer or group so try the search box to the right, or the left • you are so insanely devoted to gaming that you'll work for what we can pay you, so just keep reading • you are interested • you are on the telephone, writing furiously and holding a finger up to tell the person who just came into your office to hold on a second • you are good or think you are and need some exposure; we may be able to provide it • you are still telling the database to do a lot of unnecessary work • you are not required to repair it at your station • you are required to attend 24 hours per week • you are not terribly concerned about how people will perform your work 50 years from now • you are basically in a class by yourself • you are given enough time at school to complete your work • you are ready to go! • you are telling me that nothing is true and everything is permitted? • you are extremely proud of our 30 years of having an outstanding reputation • you are ready and we'll make a broadcaster out of you yet

(cut out of the final edit by some guy using a PowerBook)

(being completely irrational)

you are a liar, a spoiled child, a troll • you are not going to see any more e-mail litigation • you are knee-deep in it • "you are there!" Often, however, software makers don't even need to advertise these "remote monitoring" capabilities, which allow network administrators to peek at an employee's screen in real time, scan data files and e-mail at will, tabulate keystroke speed and accuracy, overwrite passwords and even seize control of a remote workstation, if they find it necessary • you are essentially leaving a trail of virtual bread crumbs for the telcos, visa and law enforcers • you are tired • you are Joan Benoit or Carlos Lopes • you are running and are feeling that relaxed, floating "I could run forever" feeling, try to focus on your mental picture of that effort • you are undecided • you are obliged to be intimate with them? what if you don't fall within their preference column? are they going to fink you out to the other campers? "Oh, don't bother getting to know that person" • you are taking some hard-ass math class like Trig or something of course Trig wasn't that hard, but just pretend that it was • you are told that you will receive a graphing calculator for Christmas • you are forbidden to open it until Christmas day • you are feeling disempowered • you are having difficulties expressing yourself or getting your point across

(the wrong answer on the multiple choice section of the LSAT)

you are applying yourself • you are not able to finish each section without a certain amount of guessing • you are sometimes given irrelevant material, but don't dismiss it until you've actually assessed it in terms of what you've been asked • you are saying that you've managed to combine Buzzy's food with hospital food? The Jell-o is a zesty tingly jello, not like the common bland-tasting jellos • you are a boring educational show being broadcast to other kids' living rooms • you are right, 90% of the questions were along the lines of, "The Three Stooges are the best! Question mark" • you are bored with driving and I am weary of lecturing • • you are preparing to sit quietly in neat rows for long periods of time doing exactly what you are told as an adult • you are ready to feign interest in their tedious jabber • you are slouching • you are doing?" asked Red Riding Hood • you are both synchronized with the universe or something • you are lazy, untalented losers, unfit to kiss the feet of a genius like Friedrich Nietzsche • you are reasonably confident that you can do significantly better on the second attempt • you are no longer even sure that you're practicing the right game

(feeling quite overwhelmed you must say)

you are a failure • you are able to divine how people are feeling about you • you are continually on trial to prove that your opinions and actions are correct • you are not upset • you are finding this situation can go on for weeks, months or even years • you are actually distorting your memories of the past • you are seriously thinking this way at present, let me state the message of this chapter loud and clear: you are wrong in your belief that suicide is the only solution or the best solution to your problem • you are walking into a trap with yawning jaws • you are never going to fit everything in and oh! What about the "gaps"? • you are a concrete person so I'm going to figure that you wouldn't mind a pre-planned lesson for your son • you are not a fighter alone who's mission is to beat everybody up on his path to save his girlfriend • you are about to play, the level is being loaded in the background • you are more knowledgeable than I had anticipated! Good, good • you are a sadist who just wants to read it and laugh hysterically at me • you are utterly incapable of feeling or understanding what you have been doing to me for so long • you are drawn to me, you cannot help but come near • you are frightened, I can hear it in your breath • you are not to blame • you are there, you have reached your peak • you are finding this too difficult

(exactly what they're looking for and that should frighten you)*

you are not supposed to spread your legs in a short dress, or she's some sort of fashion pioneer • you are bored • you are feeling bored • you are still bored • you are trying to find out how we see black holes • you are the smartest smart person I've ever known • you are at it • you are going to have a hard time finding it • you are looking for it and who has time to go through all of that anyway? • you are willing to share • you are looking for a great book, take a look at some book • you are up to? According to? • you are reading now • you are willing • you are dealing with the situation • you are or what you want to accomplish in the world • you are going to have to define your interests a little better before I can help you • you are contributing to something • you are planning to take a year off • you are only spelling out a single plausible scenario • you are not simply describing the year's most fashionable cliché • you are probably appalled • you are better off investing your energies elsewhere in the first place • you are about to be treated with more respect than you might be accustomed to • you are just after the money; just say that the other offer, taken as a whole, is attractive and more financially feasible • you are famous • you are allowed to publish

(the significant answer in an inkblot test)*

you are a chosen one which means you are a golden/seeker your primary sub-type is defined by "golden" characteristics and your secondary sub-type is defined by "seeker" characteristics • you are no fair-weather friend? • you are applying knowledge outside of its usual context • you are a talented, versatile greeting card artist who has lots of ideas for Christmas cards and box designs, then you're the person they need

(well on your way)*

you are not finding it very difficult to grow and change tend to be
controlling of others are naïve and too trusting of others have
trouble committing to others are too kind and let people take
advantage of you find it very difficult to open up to others are
judgmental and intolerant of others become depressed and
pessimistic can be selfish and demanding of others when you are
in love fall quickly for someone but fall out of love quickly too
enjoy exploring your partner's thoughts and emotions will fall
for a strong person easily try to show only your good side and
keep your faults to yourself are hard to catch but are prone to get
serious quickly when caught ignore problems and remain hope-
ful that things will get better pick your partner carefully are will-
ing to wait for a quality person hope this is the perfect partner
you've been dreaming of need to always feel appreciated, special
and unique quicky adapt to your partner's mood and lifestyle are
looking for a forever love, someone who will bond are very
guarded until you can trust your partner in friendships keep the
conversation going late into the night tend to be the most popu-
lar person you know are now hanging on by a very thin thread •
you are the class of September 11 and we do not lack for examples

(the space between the heavens and the corner of some foreign field)

you are going to create something of this ilk, you should really be doing it on your own • you are saying and I am going to do a lot of this on my own but I also believe in doing something right the first time and the best way to do something right is to get a lot of collaboration from the start • you are viewing this page in a single window • you are lost in a haze of alcohol soft middle age the pie in the sky turned out to be miles too high and you hide hide hide behind brown and mild eyes • you are dead safe in the permanent gaze of a cold, glass eye • you are sleeping with your new-found faith • you are still missing it; you are still winding things up too tightly • you are pretty much going to have to go with the story-line Roger used • you are going to send a copy of the script to Rog? That's the funniest thing I have heard yet on these forums • you are in favour of this idea • you are thinking there is a story

(rendered completely useless)

you are always the first one to hear something in the distance (i.e., approaching car, person, storm) • you are found in the fantasy/SF section • you are the definition of "weird" • you are fascinated with language, linguistics, theology, anthropology, slang, subculture and the madness of crowds • you are trying to say you are eccentric, very intelligent or crazy, but you think that you are normal and they are the ones who are odd • you are frequently offered "Santa's helper" jobs at Christmas without an interview • you are on drugs • you are half asleep and half awake, the worlds tend to blur and you can see numerous realities existing at once • you are right in the sense that the public does own the airwaves, although, the last time I checked this same public was not current in making payments to this system • you are undertaking its renovation

(a B- grade on a C paper)

you are absent, you are absent • you are there and are not paying attention • you are absent for some legitimate reason like illness, jury duty, a death in the family, etc. • you are absent for a legitimate reason but you are still absent and will not receive the full benefit of the missed class nor will the class benefit from your participation • you are responsible for the content of all lectures, discussions and any changes announced in class even if you are absent • you are absent which is why you are having trouble with class work • you are unsure what constitutes cheating • you are probably not making a productive contribution to the class and will probably not be earning full credit • you are absent • you are not here, you can't contribute anything or demonstrate your sincerity, so frequent absences will harm your participation grade • you are not here, you will also miss chances to work on your writing in class, to glean insight from discussion, etc. • you are not familiar with computers, go to the computer lab (building 2, room 405) as soon as possible • you are absent during an in-class freewriting assignment, two points will be deducted from your final grade • you are continually absent, I will ask you to withdraw from the course • you are late, make sure that I have you marked down as present or your will be marked as absent NB I take attendance at the beginning of class • you are not doing something worthwhile • you are told otherwise • you are not required to meet with me outside of class meetings, I advise you to attend a few of my office hours to discuss your writing and any questions you may have about the course material • you are told otherwise, your papers should have the same format • you are really sick, or when you have a real emergency, you are absent • you are a cell phone user, as a courtesy to me and to your fellow students, please switch off your cell phone during class or absent yourself from the room • you are generally expected to tow the company line, agree with the teacher and the text • you are expected to have many reference sources, especially those unknown to your instructor how else are they going to learn anything! In college your instructor hopes you will disagree with them and come armed with unusual, credible books with which to back your forceful rhetoric during break time • you are expected read far more than the assignments, do extra research, get to class before time and it is sometimes desirable to make friends and even work your way into the department • you are not careful you can end up like one person I talked with who couldn't even get into medical school in Grenada with his grades and courses, nor any other "offshore" institutions • you are disappointed with your grade, don't come to me and ask what's wrong with it because you were absent

(so beautiful to me)*

you are so beautiful • you are so beautiful • you are so beautiful •
you are so beautiful artist: Babyface • you are so beautiful • you
are so beautiful, yes you are to me you are so beautiful you are to
me can't you see? • you are so beautiful the lyrics are the property
of their respective authors, artists and labels • you are so beauti-
ful • you are so beautiful • you are so beautiful artist: Ray Charles
• you are so beautiful • you are so beautiful • you are so beautiful
to me • you are so beautiful • you are so beautiful • you are so beau-
tiful • you are so beautiful to meee • you are so beautiful, would
you please • you are so beautiful the lyrics are the property of their
respective authors, artists and labels • you are so beautiful to
artist: Joe Cocker • you are so beautiful to me you are so beauti-
ful to me • you are so beautiful from Joe Cocker • you are so
beautiful • you are so beautiful • you are so beautiful to me you
are so beautiful to me can't you see you're everything I hoped for
• you are so beautiful has been visited 127 times • you are so beau-
tiful to me • you are so beautiful to me • you are so beautiful to me
• you are so wonderful to me can't you see you're everything I
hoped for • you are so beautiful to me the hottest songs from Joe
Cocker • you are so beautiful • you are so beautiful to me • you are
the lyrics • you are so beautiful to me @ googlesearch, you are so
beautiful to me @ msnsearch Joe Cocker – you are so beautiful to
me @ yahoosearch Joe Cocker – you are so beautiful to me @
looksmartsearch, you are so beautiful to me @ asksearch, you are
so beautiful to me @ AOL • you are so beautiful to me belongs to
the writer or performer of Joe Cocker – you are so beautiful, if you
want to use Joe Cocker – you are so beautiful to me, please contact
the writer or performer of Joe Cocker – you are so beautiful • you
are so beautiful to me • you are so beautiful to me • you are so
beautiful to me • you are so beautiful to me letras Joe Cocker –
you are so beautiful to me song lyrics Joe Cocker – you are so
beautiful to me song text Joe Cocker – you are so beautiful to me
paroles Joe Cocker – you are so beautiful to me • you are so

beautiful to me • you are so beautiful to me you are so beautiful to me you are so beautiful to me • you are just not sure what there is left to say • you are so beautiful • you are so beautful to me if you find some error in you are so beautiful, would you please

(unconsciously acting upon your cultural biases)

you are perceived as being part of the problem or may not have the credibility required • you are a potential target for political attack and robbery • you are not with a man, you are free game; every woman was harassed • you are arrested and subject to torture • you are guilty until proven innocent in many foreign countries and few countries provide a jury trial • you are not used to the currency • you are trying to blend in • you are more apt to meet people from your host country if you are not a part of "Team USA" • you are not interested in job ideas, it is valuable to know that there are members of the extended Bates family throughout the world who would enjoy talking with you • you are on the front lines of the teaching staff • you are at the limits of your knowledge • you are responsible for filling and shaping that time • you are in a better position to see how well they are doing • you are familiar with required laboratory procedures, safety precautions and equipment and emergency procedures • you are to work together to achieve the desired outcomes • you are perceived as being part of the problem or may not have the credibility required to influence others • you are sure to find some things that are so good that you will want to accept them for yourself • you are just as sure to find other things of which you disapprove • you are on an equal footing • you are not forcing them to go against the Tapu of their people • you are pregnant and poor and have to drive 500 miles to the nearest abortion clinic? Why does everyone assume you are incapable of thinking about anything more profound than nail polish and "preschool jitters"? With so much new media out there by women and for women, why is no one addressing serious questions? Prose continues: "There's plenty of advice on how to change ourselves – woman by woman, pound by pound, wrinkle by wrinkle – but not a shred of guidance on how to change our situation" • you are wondering, this type of mental discipline is very difficult because it runs counter to our brain's wish to simplify things and jump to conclusions •

you are an authority figure, he will respect you and agree with everything you say • you are below him in power, he will either ignore you completely or make repeated attempts to discredit you in front of others whom he is trying to impress • you are more likely to obey him than if he was wearing jeans and a sweater • you are dealing with human subjects • you are travelling and you are travelling and that's it

(a game of tic-tac-toe that kicked the shit out of the Pentagon computers)*

you are an American or have sent a message like "Virginia, the Afghan rug is unravelling" • you are on CIA/CIFA/FBI/DIA/NSA camera! • you are white! The daou of poo [updated] the rape of the Lockean my gift to progressive firebrand Jane Hamsher and crack donk cyberflack Josh Marshall, as background music for their growing conspiracy-fuelled dementia and with special thanks to David Bowie tortured reasoning a few quick thoughts on "Cheney's Chappaquiddick" a fourth brief conversation with my sexy new rimless glasses "senior Chinese officials slam Communist party censorship Hume interviews Cheney the cover-up is bigger than the crime even when the crime is smaller than a crime Iraq's WMD: what would you have done? • you are dead, a philosophical meditation/Andy Garcia tribute post it's been three days after a particularly unpleasant bus ride, a shy and timid young gentleman named Willard finally comes into his own a protein wisdom microfiction identity politics are great and all, just so long as they, y'know, don't get too uppity the new, less "pedantic" protein wisdom: post number four Gore assails domestic wiretapping program my first brief conversation with the ghost of Shelley Winters one of the biggest no-names in the world they call him al-Flipper, al-Flipper • you are dead a philosophical meditation my fourth brief conversation with the 2 mg regimen of Klonopin clonazepam prescribed me by my GP Iran/Iran so far away or, A Flock of Seegullibles • you are not feeling all that great, but • you are pre-sentient mass of cells, this country will protect you and your rights to the nth degree • you are frying on Quality X • you are planning on spamming, don't bother • you are excited • you are asking – you know, this window opened up where, for the first time, really, in 40 years or so, the country was paying attention to the moral issue of what we should do about people who live in poverty • you are busy • you are a black chief, don't you say to the troops "Hey, you know what, you knuckleheads? If a tape comes up of one of you beating the dogshit out of a black guy, I'm going to be kind of pissed" • you are right about that • you are saying • you are just catching this because somebody had a camera, and that this is just some little corner of an overall picture that's happening all over • you are looking for honesty and efficiency • you are at a table with a woman who was not your wife … and again, like that, he just said "Well, I like pretty women, Mike, don't you?" [laughter] [applause] so you either love that or hate it • you are watching, if you are watching on a Friday night, we're live • you are going to do it? I think that's ultimately ridiculous • you are in a deep, deep hole here • you are sitting there, you know, having this experience surrounded by fax machines and squawk boxes • you are a guy who paints a big canvas when you do a novel • you are absolutely right • you are not sure that she'll do your bidding on abortion • you are sure to find an addictive diversion • you are playing your hole cards, 4th, 5th, 6th, and 7th • you are dealt the same kinds of hole cards • you are used to it

(on your way to the store to get a litre of milk)*

you are opening the can while your head is wedged in a horse's ass • you are all being played for chumps! Alright, now give me your paw • you are left with a gross, sticky mess • you are having trouble with the pronounciation, it's: cuitlacoche kweet-lah-koh-chay or huitlacoche dat-sfuckin-nas-tee • *You Are Going To Prison* by Jim Hogshire • you are wondering why I didn't actually make this stuff in my toilet – give me a break • you are going to prison • you are done editing, the tiddler is created • you are connected or not • you are looking forward to the immediate benefit of a happier, less gassy, less itchy, less fussy baby • you are nearing the end of the checkout process? No sales tax • you are out, a cheaper manual breast pump may be sufficient • you are on-the-go, it makes a perfect healthy alternative to a quick meal

(the weak argument in an elaborate doctoral thesis)

you are Laura from *Little House on the Prairie* • you are Beethoven • you are grandfather as a young boy • you are one of the relatives that came from Virginia • you are baby Verdi • you are important to us • you are the best possible explanation • you are trying to collect pieces that make sense of these different puzzles [many different interpretations and explanations depending on the society and culture you belong to] • you are required to go over throughout the year • you are interested over Christmas break • you are writing an informal journal and your intuition tells you not to worry about writing quality • you are expected to be literate and serious about your work • you are serious about doing well • you are interested, say so! If you have done work in this area, say so! If you are interested in a particular program, say so! And explain why you are interested! Keep it short, though • you are willing to go to another part of the country • you are the type of person who will lose steam • you are not accepted, etc. • you are getting back at Fletcher • you are trying to make up for lost time • you are not quite sure how to respond • you are ready to let someone else read it

(your 19th century procurer)*

you are reading, please don't run! I write this completely inde-
pendent of their other merits and demerits, but it's been slightly
corrosive for American democracy • you are a pimp – that's a
compliment • you are interested in reading some Austen and
haven't before, I would recommend you read *Persuasion* first as it
is the quickest read and, in some ways, the most fulfilling I know
that's subjective! • you are susceptible to injury, or you are just not
really into running a lot • you are glad to know that admitted
terrorists may be required to be interviewed by a consular officer!
Actually, even if you answer "No" to all these questions you still
have to show up • you are recovered for the big day, so be it • you
are "going out for tea" or "you will meet for tea"; this will likely
refer to a traditional English-style afternoon tea, tea or coffee,
scones, cucumber sandwiches, floral decorations on the china,
etc. • you are correct from a classical viewpoint • you are right
about the pun; and this has puzzled me, since it seems to be a
visual pun for those who see the name written, and thus wasted
on those who hear the name spoken on stage • you are an ass, you
are an ass • you are sorry, CNN • you are currently signed in as
nobody • you are talking about our ever-evolving English
language – especially slang – who would know better than some-
one involved in the same type of community as the person who
used the phrase? Yes, we all run the risk of finding someone who
simply feels like "f*cking with us," but isn't that what slang does
to the English language anyway? At this point, anything I say here
would be redundant • you are still reading, get in touch, and I'll
send you a fruitcake by way of appreciation

(not but let's say you are)*

you are feeling suicidal now, please stop long enough to read this
• you are reading this page • you are here because you are troubled
and considering ending your life • you are thinking about it, you
feel pretty bad • you are still alive at this minute • you are still a
little bit unsure • you are not a bad person, or crazy, or weak, or
flawed, because you feel suicidal • you are not acting on it • you
are feeling something • you are going to live

(your favourite letter of the alphabet except H)*

you are here for the first time, we're sure this is not what you had expected to find • you are back to refresh yourself on aspects of writing texts more likely to get printed, read below • you are 13 • you are not letting him get much sleep, and I can see why when I look at the data charts • you are stealing the show • you are most welcome • you are not supposed to be worried about them at all right now, you'll be doing plenty of that when they are in their late 60s, if not sooner, hopefully not • you are two and understand calculus before you hit kindergarten, what can you do? It's kind of a nasty world right now, but there are safe pockets, so you are in a good place • you are beautiful and you have a beautiful name • you are the young man who can't spell "fuck" • you are one smart fucker • you are unable to view some languages clearly • you are about • you are not trying hard enough • you are under oath • you are honest about this topic, you will acknowledge that Arabs aren't the only ones entitled to self-determination • you are not, we won't be nice back

(an asshole)

you are a big floaty asshole, that's what you are, you dumb shit [post a response]• you are really a hopeless asshole [post a response]• you are really a hopeless asshole [post a response] • you are already a minister for the environment, you are not bothered about the environment haze and yet you got the guts to announce the hike in assessment rates • you are allowed to change the subject: [post a response] • you are really a hopeless asshole name: e-mail: subject: comments: [post a response] • you are most likely to say: "I'll be back" • you are dumb? Yeah: [post a response] • you are an asshole – song parodies for you! • you are an asshole tonight • you are using today will be able to play this song for you, once you have unzipped it • you are an asshole and don't you try to blame it on me, you deserve all the credit, you are an asshole tonight • you are an asshole tonight and I've got a feeling, you'll be an asshole the rest of your life • "you are right" • you are an asshole tonight

(last documented in the Earl of Derby's private collection in 1723)*

you are mine, saith the Lord • you are not from New York – I'm
generalizing, certainly not all New York writers are like this • you
are pretty funny • you are and it's mobbed with people • you are
writing novels, you have so much to do that you never have to
worry • you are always trying to take things out • you are a couple
of kids pulling a scam in your back bedroom, you probably don't
want to give that impression • you are doing the ripping • you are
making me blush • you are stalking me so intently you can't wait
for an update • you are led into wild errors about the nature of the
society • you are more of a simple-minded person, you can still
wrap your thoughts around certain things that Socrates ques-
tions that today still have no specific definitions • you are talking
to yourself • you are my love • you are my prisoner • you are just a
tease, aren't you? Jabberwacky: sure am • you are the bastard • you
are reading at the moment, and do you have anything in particular
to recommend to encompass visitors? At the moment I am reading
three books at once, *I Saw Ramallah*, a memoir by Mourid
Barghouti, an exiled Palestinian writer, and *The Whale Caller* by
the South African writer Zakes Mda – this one is not out yet, it
will be out in a couple of weeks, I got it as complimentary from
the publisher • you are already assuming that Africans should
only write about their roots and identity – you forget that their
roots, like everyone else's, are the human root, and their identity
is the human identity, and so they run no danger of losing their
roots and identity as long as they live among humans

(billed as the nicotine patch to the world)*

you are just as guilty as the rest of our society • you are entitled to your opinion • you are in this incompassionate mob of people that consider yourselves to be the healthy-elite-purists of the world • you are quoting someone else here, but what about flight attendants? • you are 100 percent wrong if you think otherwise

(everything you want in a drugstore)*

you are looking for raw material • you are able and willing to pay the prices asked • you are not careful filling the tank, but no worse than any of the others • you are supporting a Filipino child for a month • you are nice or buy one • you are right, though – this has nothing to do with political affiliation • you are really crazy when you are on a first-name basis with everyone • you are being lied to, here is another engrossing and infuriating compilation of muckraking articles, exposés and provocative claims

(only as good as the next guy)

you are down 3 units • you are down 2 units • you are not winning enough constantly • you are wiped out! So even betting "don't" is bad • you are laying $10 to win $5 • you are reading article 26 • you are to wonderful, I couldn't possibly accept this – no thank you • you are equally bad if not worse • you are having a delicious Thanksgiving dinner – bring me that golden delicious turkey or you are fired! Man: but sir!?! It's Thanksgiving • you are at the end of article 26 • you are getting bogged down with all the other things of disobey • you are indeed interested in the rest of what disobey has to offer, you have two options: go to • you are in a chatroom for long enough, eventually some bastard working for some bastard company logs in and starts taking down names • you are reading the mail so they put you on more lists • you are a volunteer, a youth leader, a youth pastor or the pope – you can use these practical tools to help your ministry • you are going to start exercising and if you are really going to put that much mayo on your burger! • you are really into it, move to Nashville • you are going to play the game, you've got to go where they're swinging the bats … so move here, get a job, learn to drive with these people at 5 pm • you are a copywriter, when did your love of words start? I am a Canadian-Hungarian • you are after me

(the eggman)

you are not familiar, Pete Shotton was Lennon's closest boyhood pal, an original member of the Quarrymen until John broke the washboard over Pete's head! And a close friend and confidant of John's to the very end • you are he we are all spirits of the same god as you are me and we are all together therefore we are all the same see how they run like pigs from a gun man on earth today for the most part see how they fly denies this simple beautiful truth I'm crying that they do is a sad thing sitting on a cornflake, cookie-cutter conformist capitalists waiting for the van to come that take carpools to work corporation T-shirt, stupidly all dressed the same, in their boring bloody Tuesday day-to-day jobs man you been a naughty boy and criticize people like John Lennon you let your face grow long who don't look like they do I am the eggman I am a spirit of God they are eggmen and so are you I am the walrus I am God and therefore so are you goo goo a' joob isn't that wonderful? Return to the start • you are not familiar, Pete Shotton was Lennon's closest boyhood pal, an original member of the Quarrymen until John broke the washboard over Pete's head! And a close friend and confidant of John's to the very end • you are he we are all spirits of the same god as you are me and we are all together therefore we are all the same see how they run like pigs from a gun man on earth today for the most part see how they fly denies this simple beautiful truth I'm crying that they do is a sad thing sitting on a cornflake, cookie-cutter conformist capitalists waiting for the van to come that take carpools to work corporation T-shirt, stupidly all dressed the same, in their boring bloody Tuesday day-to-day jobs man you been a naughty boy and criticize people like John Lennon you let your face grow long who don't look like they do I am the eggman I am a spirit of God they are eggmen and so are you I am the walrus I am God and therefore so are you goo goo a' joob isn't that wonderful? [end of file] (shovelling shit in a Roman stable)[†]

you are hereby invited to avoid reading this book linearly • you are no financial genius • you are also going to have to agree to take in a few old people to your house since there's no way to pay them their promised benefits as well • you are just blowing smoke • you are basically spouting Communist rhetoric • you are a hack • you are proving that this is a country rampant with the soft bigotry of low expectations • you are an Xer and would be well advised to find yourself a nice lawless, taxless tropical island fiefdom somewhere and open a bar on the beach and those of you adept at witchcraft may want to consider turning yourselves into porcupines those needles will come in handy • you are givin' it to us so straight like that! Anyway, it's like what they'd accuse us of doin' • you are absolutely right, they will never get the evidence they need to say: "This is the one God for sure! This is not just any God whose countenance I have experienced! This is the one, the only one! And I would know if there were such another as this! Nothing can outshine this one God! I know that for sure!" ... and she looked at the others, wide-eyed with the discovery • you are a priest, scion of some illustrious family or other, you want to go to your local temple and worship some humongous icon of a god crafted by the local artists and stonemasons? You want to affirm your position as gatekeeper? But lo and behold, what have we here, along side the rest? A gigantic statue of the grandson, a prole? The common man, made good, I might add! • you are at that point when • "you are interested in what's true, you are makin' the discovery that you happen to be in love, right Jack?" and the other breathed a sigh of relief and put his face in his hands • you are perceived as a threat • "you are almost made to feel weird if you even mention it," says West, a resident of Edmonds, Washington • you are worried about offending anyone with a seasonal greeting, try this pro forma hello from Australia's leading pusillanimous politically correct puffbucket premier • you are accepting these terms • you are wrong there • you are sure to provoke multiple discussions, ranging from child labour to parity in workplace safety and including catchy terms like "dumping," "outsourcing" and "brain drain" • you are able to read their components: what six-year-old could distinguish between "phonograph" and "photograph" without sounding out each word's second syllable? And yet, despite the obvious superiority of rigorous training – whether in phonics or anything else – successful methods are not always acknowledged • you are not always going to have a clear-cut battle of good vs. evil • you are digging yourself deeper and deeper with every post • you are a "bad" actor • you are too young, child • you are projecting a bit, no? • you are the one making such characterizations as if any of us needed that • you are having a bad day and ... • you are with me and I don't want you sitting there either • you are going to dress in drag – for whatever reason – so let me give you a little advice • you are going to shave your legs, don't be fooled by all those girly girly advertisements for aloe-enriched moisturizing gel creams • you are a man and your shaved legs need to be manly • you are ready for the razor • you are doing this • you are wrong • you are up early if I believe the 6 am time on the e-mail • you are awakened, all is understood, no strivings are required; things of the Samskrita [world of cause and effect] are not of this nature; charity practised with the idea of form Rupa may result in a heavenly birth, but it is like shooting an arrow against the sky, when the force is exhausted the arrow falls on the ground • you are observing, but things do not make much sense in this raw state • you are still interested – please reply with some personal background including your birthday • you are messing things up • you are cooking up breakfast in the kitchen and your roommate can't cut off your fingersif you "borrowed" his CDs when you moved out, among other silly things • you are not in a position to do much about it • you are eating, but is it safe to consume? • you are back to barter • you are paid for and developed by theft • you are using right now

• you are benefiting by what you keep claiming is theft • you are an honest and sincere person, you ought to avoid all possible benefits from what you claim is theft • you are extremely patient • you are that blacksmith, horse trainer, farmer or bookseller • you are able to operate without that kind of selfishness • you are a politician: O, I can see the TV commercial now – "Kevin says he's for failure" • you are not going to say that ownership is natural, which is an impossible argument, you've got to justify why and how people can "own" something • you are using the Bible to define marriage; doesn't that mean you should be against all non-Christian marriages, atheists, Jews and pagans alike? Somehow they never are • you are against gay marriage in any capacity, then I guess you'll gladly go back to being taxed as two separate people with no dependents, right? • you are willing to pay, but do you voluntarily skip deductions? Is that typical behaviour on the part of most taxpayers? • you are caught red-handed, which already "costs" the government • you are healthy, you are just a source of profit to exploitative insurance companies • you are saying that the ability to fail is what keeps the large corporations from taking over the world • you are fully aware that a corporation's sole motive is to maximize profits and thus their corporate value • you are exchanging gold bars; money requires, at some point, the "threat of force" to ensure its value • you are much happier not owning the big scary corporations you consider so invulnerable • you are willing to argue that a nondemocratic government is by definition totally illegitimate but you can't point to elections as the one differentiating factor between that monopoly and others • you are presumptively not initiating force or fraud against anyone • you are a Christian, right or left, so where does that leave us and how far do you extend that when it comes to taxation? Seriously • you are a Christian, right or left, where does that leave us and how far do you extend that when it comes to taxation? "Slaves obey your masters" – that's in there too, as in "Never let a woman teach or have authority" • you are a hypocrite if you use the Internet, if that's any comfort • you are happy to make use of the Internet, whose development was paid for by taxation, yet you don't want to actually pay your share • you are arguing for the military-industrial complex and arguing against it being wasteful of resources • you are a "progressive" after all • you are currently signed in as nobody • you are not paid to have an opinion even though you may have a forced suspension of judgment • you are right • you are going to go down the drain • you are an irreplaceable interlocutor • you are giving up any sense of future financial security in your old age so that Bush can run this unwinnable war into the unforeseeable future • you are just blowin' smoke up my skirt • you are deeply emoting, but even so, the analogy troubles me • you are the same Karen who posted on another Melanie Phillips thread that you wanted society to give your husband a job that would enable you to stay at home and look after your children • you are not thinking straight • you are wrong, Americans are very interested in Dalrymple's ideas • you are right • you are surprised that the US faces the same kind of social attacks from the left as the UK • you are naïve • you are far too apocalyptic, Caroline, which ruins your case – Britain is not the darkest corner of the deepest pit, with the sunny uplands reserved for all others • you are correct when you say they are not very socialist, however • you are not in the least interested in finding out if your theories are actually true by getting a real job in the business world and seeing how things really work • you are correct, Chuck Bird, that since Roe vs. Wade abortion has not been illegal and that 40 million abortions have taken place • you are totally brilliant and have saved me the work of responding to many of Rob Maynard's "airy-fairy" notions of the world as he sees it from his ivory tower • you are talking about or talking to • you are in Cuba to wonder at the miracles wrought by Castro, why not stop off in Miami and see why it's every Cuban's dream to stop off in Miami – and never go back? BTW, if offered a green card, how many Chileans and Nicaraguans do you think would turn it down? Yeah • you are greatly enamoured? It used to be that the socialists in the West argued that capitalism was bad because it made everyone but a few people poorer • you are greatly enamoured? The welfare state is not rising • you are a troll • you are a "dumb savage"? Hard to say, but certainly comprehensive schools do have bullying on a scale never before imagined • you are a victim of your educational opportunity

(dead now, so shut up!)

you are now reading the typing of Jay Resop • you are probably wondering what exactly is going on • you are in charge? • you are too lazy to go and read it all as I'm sure most of you are • you are free • you are free to do as we tell you • you are vacationing in France with your gay friend to avoid those awkward hospital visits • you are going to be walking to that dentist appointment • you are not going to get fired over a little three-week no-call-no-show • you are so tanked that you take yourself off the market and want to cuddle exclusively with your new friend • you are going to have a shitty few months, my friend • you are not the one • you are going about this all wrong • you are a dog on a leash like a pig in a pen • you are a Taurus and you just skipped straight to your sign, that makes sense • you are only doing that 'cause you couldn't beat me head to head • you are facing two opponents who are allied in their attempts to destroy you • you are thinking I wrote this because my personal feelings have been hurt, think again

(in the process of being palimpsested)*

you are trying to impress the audience with the density of some-thing, or otherwise make a point that specifically requires dense and unreadable text • you are republishing what you are posting and why you couldn't have just rewritten it in your own words • you are helping the copyright holder; often it's not that hard to ask permission • you are better prepared to take affirmative actions of mechanical and cultural control – building and starving them out of your collection • you are documenting current efforts • you are prepared • you are getting the word out to others • you are not doing it right, you damn well know you are doing it wrong, but you carry on anyway because you are too lazy to set it up to do it right after you've realized that there is a potential problem? I concluded that it must have been the mould spores • you are near a platform • you are in the cellar • you are on the ground, walk to the location you want to go to once you are above the ground and say the word again • you are not blocking the projection • you are nervous, the pointer dramatically magnifies the shaking of your hand • you are conducting an orchestra or something • you are not nervous, it still jiggles unpleasantly • you are addressing this very problem at the same time, aren't you? Amazing how multi-purpose these tips can be • you are running behind, skip a slide, or gloss over one, or talk a bit faster, or don't accept questions • you are a famous poet or novelist reading your own work, what is the point? • you are not colourful either • you are being stupid, reveal what it says

(an incestuous mess)*

you are rich!!!!! posted by: rob posted on: Dec 14 views: 535 re: nudity oh my gosh! dude, you should of stopped it at the point when she grabbed your penis • you are in a world of trouble and don't recognize it • you are still lying • you are aware of something bothering you; you may have found a solution to your sleep problem • you are safe in dreams • you are alive again or you wake up • you are suffering from night terrors • you are a Democratic candidate for Minnesota's 6th Congressional district • you are something quite different aren't you? Why are you hiding this information? I do not question your right to your opinion but suggest that you should disclose exactly who you are and that you try to be more original • you are not elected, but it looks like a you'd fit right into that den of thieves! • you are just an anonymous coward • you are the surrender monkey • you are so concerned about plagarism and original thought • you are and you try to be more original • you are talking out of both sides of your mouth, pal • you are just muddying the waters • you are the one doing the spin • you are right on the money and you have the competence and the credibility to comment on this issue • you are trolling • you are only saying that because you are afraid I'll think you are a scumbag if you tell me how you really feel • you are careful to sterilize the pubes you collect off the urinal at work before you put them in your mouth and beat off, you are certainly not going to make yourself sick • you are not turning down dates with other good-looking guys with pubes of their own, then I wouldn't describe your obsession as necessarily unhealthy • you are not hurting anyone • you are creating a hostile work environment, and he may get your pervert ass fired • you are as discreet as you are hygienic, I don't see a problem • "you are not that kind of baby, are you?" Edna asked, somewhat concerned by the boy's request • "you are the most wonderful boy! Any mother would be proud of you!" She kissed his cold cheek and held him close • you are either for us or against us • you are culpable

(available only through this limited TV offer)

you are really creating intellectual property and either assigning it, selling it or renting it • you are linked in, and you can send as well as retrieve • you are done, you "hang-up" again • you are interested in this option • you are still free to take advantage • you are checking whether the use of any information you provide is governed • you are buying our argument • you are dissatisfied • you are losing • you are entitled to declines in your last years

(the party of the first part) *

you are looking for a particular theme or product that you can't
find here

(a no-good, lazy son of a bitch)

you are really idle • you are knackered • you are pissed off • you are going to watch them, so why not entertain you by forking out the big bucks for entertaining, quality programming instead of just sticking a bunch of people on an island and turning on the TV? Isn't that their job? Isn't that their responsibility? Nope • you are not updating yourself, why the fuck should they, but that's just the attitude that they get from thinking about themselves all the time • you are completely unacceptable • you are wrong, you stupid no-good, commie-loving queer! "But I'm a peace-loving person" • you are an incompetent slob and I had to fire you? • you are insane? Maybe you are just sitting around reading *Guns and Ammo*, masturbating in your own feces, do you just stop and go "Wow! It is amazing how fucking crazy I really am?" • you are left with nothing but the mole on your back? You're probably wondering who I am talking about, huh? Well, I can't tell you • you are to come with me to Fortraan • you are not urinating in here man! Bender: Don't talk! Don't talk! It makes it crawl back up! Andrew: You whip it out and you are dead before the first drop hits the floor! Bender: You're pretty sexy when you get angry • you are a parent's wet dream • you are a neo maxi zoom dweebie • you are ready pal • you are gonna eat that? Claire: Can I eat? Bender: I don't know • you are crazy to make us write an essay telling you who we think we are (often replaced by an apostrophe)†

you are travelling with Xena, then you must be pretty brave • you
are looking for very specific rules • you are not a doctor yet, Boyd,
and until you are, why don't you keep the medical speeches to
yourself? • you are an illiterate, dyslexic teenager • you are very
lucky to have someone like Luva in your life to show you the error
of your grammatical ways, aren't you? Thank you Luva, for
teaching me • you are keen • you are feelings • you are a shrink or
an art critic – you should disregard this meaning of the word • you
are making a comparison between two or more things • you are
new to Italian lessons • you are talking about one o'clock, since
"one" is singular • you are not granted any other rights and copy-
right holders reserve all other rights • you are and you are • you
are uncertain which form to use • you are grown up enough to
have got this far so you can mark your own • you are face-to-face
or on the phone, you have the chance to reword anything that's
unclear; in an e-mail, you don't have that luxury – you have to get
it right, first time • you are familiar – and confident – with the
basics of writing; any form of writing is easy to you • you are still
feeling a little hesitant about your abilities and would like some
extra support • you are not completely happy with the quality of
support you receive • you are getting no results from your search
• you are getting results from your search • you are searching for
Bishop's Court, enter Bishops Court • you are sober • you are going
out, please be home by 10 o'clock • you are preparing to deal with
them • you are on your own here • you are a professional
phenomenologist, you can live comfortably without the word
"exists" in your vocabulary • you are outside the computer lab,
don't force it to serve double duty as a verb • you are going to
apologize, so apologize: "I'm sorry I wrote a bad poem"

(a big waste of time, for the most part)

you are about to read something that may sound a little off-the-wall • you are either: (a) wondering whether you should agree to be featured in an article on our site, or (b) you've already agreed to be featured and are eagerly anticipating your interview for your scintillating article • you are out of the house • you are unable to pay a bill immediately • you are getting bad advice from the wrong people, getting ripped off by money-hungry car stereo installers – be careful they will take you for a ride! • you are bound to make the same $3,000 mistake I made • you are of wide interest and pay a high bounty, so in most cases you can actually earn more than you would selling your space • you are already a member and would like to see a feature added; static or automatic, it makes no difference to us • you are still trying to decide whether you want to be featured or not, let us offer you some advice • you are the focal point • you are probably wondering to yourself, "What can I expect from this experience? How should I prepare?" After all, this is such a wonderful opportunity to get your name up in lights and stand centre stage on a national level • you are outside and turn the lamp off before reading anything • you are out of it • you are about to read something that may change your life in ways you've only dreamed of • you are original as your DNA • you are my best resource here; I value our relationship and need you to please find the time for this • you are bigger than they are • you are taking a big step • you are going to want to find out how easy that is to do • you are not looking in the right direction • you are looking at the wrong thing • you are expecting us to list all of your accomplishments and awards in your article, you'll be disappointed

(a poor player who struts and frets his hour upon the stage and is heard no more)*

you are making a scene • you are scared to stand up for your beliefs • you are not a prince, nor were meant to be! You are a minor character, one that will do to make a nice catch, start a rally or two, assist the manager; no doubt, an easy tool, deferential, glad to be of use • you are a member of the Republican party • you are just dying to believe something is not hard evidence, except perhaps about your state of mind • you are really a friend • you are very quite right about the fact that he is a prick and a very bad one at it too • you are well • you are on to them • you are so wise, like a miniature Buddha • you are such a fan! • you are not too offended • you are no Jack Kennedy • you are a mist that appears for a little time and then vanishes

(surely mistaken)

you are the greatest thing since chopped liver • you are coming soon! Well, I am coming sooner than you think! • you are not ready, the thought of his return may not excite you like it does me • you are the one who has to do it • you are watching and walking in tune with the spirit, you won't be in the dark • you are dying to ask • you are coming from somewhere else • you are often in my thoughts and seldom omitted in my prayers • you are his and he is yours; that he has loved you with an everlasting love and therefore in loving-kindness has drawn you to himself; that he will surely accomplish that which he has begun and that nothing which can be named or thought of shall ever be able to separate you from him • you are confused • you are sounding a little false • you are asking this, you've obviously never heard of the comic and have stumbled here in search of some wisdom and guidance from God, which you are not going to get from us and should really try praying instead of looking for him on the World Wide Web

(detachable penis)

you are an adult and you are loud and/or obnoxious, rowdy,
grouchy, grumpy, moody, rude, crude, tattooed, filthy, dirty,
stinking, sweating, bloating, belching, farting, vomiting, moshing,
bleeding, oozing with pus, coughing up blood, screaming,
yelling, ranting, stepping on toes, causing a scene, acting up,
acting out, acting bizarre, looking for trouble, spoiling for a fight,
having a bad hair day, on the rag, suffering from PMS, suffering
from halitosis, bursting with testosterone, oozing with estrogen,
anti-abortion or pretty much anti-anything, pro-choice or pretty
much pro-anything, sexually liberated, perverted, homosexual,
weird, sarcastic, unseemly, disruptive, revolutionary, rebellious,
psychotic, upset, paranoid, schizophrenic, homophobic, deranged,
gun-toting, flag-burning, patriotic, intelligent, anarchic, spon-
taneous, free-spirited, predatory, troubled, disturbed, disturbing,
an outcast, open-minded, adventurous, brave, eccentric, a poet,
an artist, an idealist, a realist, a radical, a loose cannon, waging a
personal war, crossing the lines, climbing the walls, storming the
gates, rioting, looting, waking and baking, carousing, carrying a
chip on your shoulder, a free bird, a coy dog, a vixen, a bitch, a wolf
in sheep's clothing, a sheep in wolf's clothing, a black sheep, a
shepherd, a goatherd, a scapegoat, a goat god, unpredictable,
contradictory, conscious, awake, dreaming, streaking, flaming,
wild, out of control, out of bounds, out of sight, out of your mind,
out of this world, turning on, tuning in, dropping out, wearing
sandals, barefoot, wearing a toga, not wearing anything, looking
for sex, trolling the boards, proselytizing, pimping, prostituting
yourself, standing on a soapbox, jumping on the bandwagon,
falling off the wagon, marching to the beat of a different drummer,
goose-stepping, starting a doomsday cult, forming a militia,
masturbating, having sex with an alien, breaking the law, breaking
a few commandments, butchering sacred cows, cloning sheep,
cloning sheep in order to have your own harem of sexual slaves,
concerned with things *die verboten sind*, opening a can of worms,

opening a can o' whup-ass, getting medieval, going postal, un-approved, unconventional, unexplainable, unknown, unforgiven, unattractive, undressing, a peeping Tom, a pig, an exhibitionist, a voyeur, a diva, a god/dess, a Godiva, in a gadda da vida, a harlot, a heathen, a heretic, a blasphemer, an iconoclast, a right-winger, a left-winger, a eunuch, a unicorn, a cannibal, an Orwellian, a Lovecraftian, a megalomaniac, a benevolent dictator, a peaceful warrior, a time traveller, a hermeticist, a hermit, a crazy old coot, a cultist, an occultist, a housewife, a single mother, a deadbeat dad, a serial monogamist, a bigamist, a polygamist, a polygynist, a polyandrist, a polyamorist, a polytheist, a polyester suit, a string of polo ponies, a nymphomaniac, a sadomasochist, a misogynist, a misandrist, a misanthrope, a misfit, a mindwarp, a mental patient, a moonbeam, a mad hatter, a March hare, a socialist, a singularity, a terrorist, a pornographer, an alien, a half-human half-alien hybrid, a clone, one of several clones in a harem of sexual slaves, open to suggestion be my sex slave, under hypnosis sleep, under surveillance, under wraps, in prison, an escaped convict, public enemy #1, on the FBI's 10 most wanted list, not running for public office, running for public office in order to destroy the system from within, Ralph Nader, Billy Graham, Patient Zero, Frankenstein, Dracula, Morpheus, Neo, Trinity, Cartman, Mumia, Leonard Peltier, Andy Kaufman, Satan, Beelzebub, Choronzon, Maya Angelou, Madonna, Al Sharpton, Elvis, Marilyn Monroe, Kurt Cobain, Tupac Shakur, Jim Morrison, the second gunman, Deep Throat, Jimmy Hoffa, Bigfoot, an M (therefore you think)†

you are being lied to • "you are being lied to" is a conspiracy theorist's dream come true • you are good, we give you money and if you are a dick, you are faded • "you are being manipulated" • you are looking for answers • you are missing the point! • you are looking to read this book to get the answers • you are having a problem or question that has been discussed recently • you are welcome to give useful answers and contribute to the discussion; you are expected not to ask questions • you are going to ask a question • you are probably going to be a little disappointed, since the people interviewing you are going to be aware of this book • you are doing anything wrong • you are not a developer • you are heckbent • you are definitely in need of those elements, just as you need electricity • you are monsters, cried the abbé, coming up; you ought to get busy! • you are looking for a book that goes into more detail • you are held back by negative entities or negative energies, look again • you are doing Noho with an entity of the light, you will quickly find that it will not use "should" • you are broke, hopeless and a poor helpless victim, this is going to be your world • you are projecting the play called "your life" through your decisions, beliefs and choices day by day • you are wanting a "challenge" – go for it • you are competing in a race and overtake the runner lying in second place • you are now coming first then you are completely wrong • you are behind them then they can't be last • you are clearly the weakest link • you are coming second

(the side effects of performance-enhancing drugs)

you are not only cheating yourself, but you are also cheating everyone around you • you are a big time competitive B B and your livelihood depends on it • you are not an experienced user then don't ever think of slinking back here • you are "normal" and don't have any "problem," the male potency pack will make your sex life even better – in fact it will make it awesome! • you are stuck in traffic • you are travelling with one • you are really clever and write some of the best songs • you are just borrowing from the body's energy bank • you are getting the original product that works! • you are painfully aware of the symptoms • you are reading about this • you are not 100 percent satisfied with the results

(a bad case of blue-balls)

you are a teenager with raging hormones but you are not really interested in playing a game with boobies in it • you are worried that your dad will be unhappy if he finds out you are playing a game with a hooter factor • you are his kid, you live in his joint and basically he runs the show • you are just gonna have to swallow that whole • you are interested in this game despite some visual nudity and let him know you feel you are mature enough to handle it • you are good to them, they'll be good to you • you are gonna get canned like a tuna and have more than your severance pay cut off • you are interested in the wrong impression • you are interested so don't be afraid to make your move

(boldly going where no man has gone before, but only as the disposable crew member)

you are safely on the road, I will guide you • you are unable to orient freely, but as you continue, your failures and experience will make the details appear and the forks and road crossings will be visible to you even before you reach them • you are setting the hook on a fine fish with rod number two • you are not charging someone $1500 • you are having a difficult time getting all the "chunks" rinsed away • you are all done • you are not the first one this has happened to • you are not alone • you are paralyzed by the fear of failure? Oh no! Here it comes! You are in no way expected to master the process on your first try but one thing is absolutely assured, you will never get it if you don't try • you are ready to split your strips • you are ready to go again • you are not sure it is *Arundinaria amabilis* • you are in business • you are worthier than I originally thought • you are a kind and caring person • you are just in the nick of time • you are a noble • you are allowed to join us • you are going to fight with Blaquestar, you need to demonstrate some skill • you are such a pretty young thing • you are the same as your father • you are very powerful inside, Dragundum • you are not working only for me • "you are the mysterious mage," said the other man • you are the street mage, Everblaze • you are very good at making threats • you are concerned for your father • you are not offended • you are there • you are not dead, boy • you are in yourself • you are in your mind • "you are dead!" Chapter 43 Darkfire led the group into the castle • you are unable to control me • you are confronted with a beauty of more dramatic character that takes your breath away • you are thinking of taking a ramble through the forest in search of wild things and you will be in distinguished company, from William the Norman and his son looking for their deer, to William Cobbett scornfully complaining of the poverty of the soil and the multitude of deer; or in more recent times sired Ward Grey – later Viscount Grey and President Theodore Roosevelt walking through the forest, observing the birds and comparing their notes with those of the songbirds of the United States • you are never quite sure if these are hallucinations – the imaginings of a sick mind – or if they are apparitions, like the witches • "you are meant to be," the play seems to be saying • you are sitting in a theatre waiting to see a play about a man named Macbeth • you are trying to cover the truth • you are Macbeth's enemy, how can you have left your family exposed to him? (it only makes the older man angry)

(translated into 20 different languages)*

you are in an environment where nobody speaks • you are not
sure what I mean

(not smart, just hard-working)

you are not required to accept this license, since you have not signed it • you are not responsible for enforcing compliance by third parties to this license • you are welcome to redistribute it under certain conditions; type ``show C'' for details • you are converting a C program to C++ • you are not sure where GNU CC finds the assembler it is using, try specifying ``-v'' when you run it • you are going to build the stage 3 compiler, then you might want to build only the C language in stage 2 • you are going to use C++, it's likely that you need to also install the libg ++ distribution • you are indeed running HP-Ux 8 • you are running a Unix-like shell, have a complete suite of Unix-like utilities in your path and have a previous version of GNU CC already installed, either through building it via the above installation method or acquiring a pre-built binary • you are linking with a library that contains functions for 134 17 January 1996 Chapter 5: installing GNU CC multiplication and division, you can tell GNU CC to call them directly by defining the macros mulsi3_libcall and the like • you are cross-compiling a standalone program or a program for an embedded system, then you may not need any header files except the few that are part of GNU CC and those of your program • you are building GNU CC with a previous version of GNU CC, you also should check to see if you have the newest version of the assembler • you are compiling with a version of GNU CC older than 1 • you are writing a header file that must work when included in ANSI C programs, write __type of__ instead of type of • you are compiling for • you are compiling for • you are compiling for • you are writing a header file to be included in ANSI C programs, write __inline__ instead of inline • you are lucky, everything should work properly • you are using cfront-model code, you can probably get away with C y g n u s S u p p o r t 201 using GNU CC not using -fno-implicit-templates when compiling files that ``do not include'' the member template definitions • you are on your own • you are compiling C++ programs and specifying directories explicitly, use this option first, then one of the two options above: -i/usr/local/lib/g++-include ffl on some SGI systems, when you use ``-lgl_s" as an option, it gets translated magically to ``-lgl_s - lx11_s -lc_s" • you are an experienced user of C or C++ compilers, your suggestions for improvement of GNU CC or GNU C ++ are welcome in any case • you are sending us on a wild goose chase • you are not sure why you are trying to fix it, or why your patch should be an improvement, we won't install it • you are not interested in explicitly initializing each element of the array • you are using • you are compiling, single precision may be faster than double precision • you are not optimizing • you are compiling older C++ programs that don't use exception handling • you are converting a C program to C ++ • you are not sure where GNU CC finds the assembler it is using, try specifying ``-v" when you run it • you are going to build the stage 3 compiler, then you might want to build only the C language in stage 2 • you are all set • you are going to be using a C ++ runtime library, this is where its install procedure will install its header files • you are building GNU CC with a previous version of GNU CC, you also should check to see that you have the newest version of the assembler • you are compiling with a version of GNU CC older than 1 • you are writing a header file that must work when included in ANSI C programs, write __type of__ instead of type of • you are writing a header file to be included in ANSI C programs, write __inline__ instead of inline • you are very lucky, everything should work properly • you are on your own • you are not sure whetherto state a fact or leave it out, state it! often people omit facts because they think they know what causes the problem and they conclude that some details don't matter • you are sending us on a wild goose chase • you are not interested in acuracy

(a painting bought solely for the frame)

you are pursuing antiques for the right reasons • you are satisfied then move on • you are used to using one product and it works, stick with it • you are a novice, expect to make mistakes and allow time to recognize and correct them • you are refinishing the trim on the car, go straight to step two • you are not replacing the felt P-seals, or they're in good shape, be careful not to mangle them price them at the dealer, they're expensive! • you are caught, you are charged not just with theft but sabotage and that's a one-way trip to the concentration camp and hard labour • you are more than welcome to print out this material for personal reading, but it is illegal to modify or sell it • you are free to use, modify and distribute it • you are very analytical and logical, as any good Vulcan is, but this makes you stick out like a sore thumb

(the only one who really likes it, really)*

you are in the dating scene yourself or if you have a young lady in your life who is just beginning to date, get this book! You'll thank me later • you are not convinced yet • you are the only one who will suffer if you continue to cling to something that wasn't meant to be • you are one of those girls who beats herself up for getting emotional, and for dreaming of nesting with a man and nurturing children, stop it right now! There is no guilt involved, there is no shame • you are not the best for him then he is also not the best for you • you are tempted to believe that he was really, really that busy • you are being used for money, status, your sports car, sex, your friends, whatever temporarily, and see if they still want to be around you and act just as they always did • you are too good for them or they don't deserve you • you are getting played • you are being used, you probably are • you are here: How can you tell if someone really likes you or if they are using you? • you are sitting by her and either your arm or leg "accidentally" touches hers and she doesn't move and if she does it's to scoot closer to you • you are weird for telling her • you are asking everyone • you are still in the "other people space," you don't want that • you are so sexy • you are looking into her eyes she'll stare straight into yours and never look away b/c she's so into your words, your voice, your thoughts • you are talking to her • you are here: How do you find out if a girl really likes you? • You are interested at least, I also think when a guy calls you at random times or calls you a few times a day just to say hi, means that he is interested • you are wearing a necklace he'll move closer and grab it to "look at the necklace" or he'll play with a tie on your shirt or a ring • you are not talking he'll just look at you and smile • you are going to the movies he'll choose a scary movie over a comedy or anything else • you are in a bad mood he will try anything to make you smile • you are crowds away • you are talking to or about another guy • you are a girl, you know if a guy likes you or not • you are having a convo • you are just joking around about it • you are here: What are signs

171

a guy likes you that you might be missing? • you are working the whole "model thing" now? That's flirting, right? • you are a person who enjoys a slightly satisfying phone relationship, talk on! • you are great • you are not supposed to call guys, but I call guys all the time because I don't care! • you are changing the primordial impulses that drive all of human nature • you are the chosen one • you are one of the Nine, ladies! I can't say it loud enough: you, the superfox reading this book, are worth asking out

(not a machine)

you are an action movie – the set also includes one ceiling attachment and hardware • you are new to Christian music and can honestly say *Pet Shop* is definitely one of the greatest albums you can buy • you are in the book • you are on the air • you are caller number nine! • you are and what you want, so at the sound of the tone, please hang up • you are listening to it later, except for you I guess it's now, like, when you are listening to it • you are the phone company, I already sent the money • you are my parents, please send money • you are my financial aid institution, you didn't lend me enough money • you are my friends, you owe me money • you are a female, don't worry, I have plenty of money • you are a customer • you are a customer, you have plenty of money and are all set

(corn, but we call it maize)

you are pushed into interior regions immediately • you are following the left or right wall! To completely nitpick this subject into abeyance, I must add that there is a fourth choice: follow the slide but ignore the shortcut path beneath it • you are near the goal, but you may be wrong • you are on the edge of the field • you are drinking good stuff • you are seeing anybody? FYI, I very, very rarely see anybody now at all • you are on your own again • you are in Wal-Mart • you are less likely to find that your husband has run off with a chippie in the UK • you are unforgivably ugly and you live in a trailer • you are unchuffed or dischuffed if something gets your back up • you are in the picture and you know where it is you want to be, it's not too difficult to go and find it," Marshall pointed out • you are running, it must be because you are running from something, but also because I was wearing shorts • you are used to it, it's almost nothing, you know, but it doesn't stop us saying "Oh gosh, it's too hot!" I'll tell you what, Steve, if you've got a week off, maybe in the next month or so, why don't you fly out and join me for a few days? Yours, S :) I'd love to do that, I'd love to do that! But, unfortunately it sounds too hot and I haven't actually got a week off in the, in the for-see-able – although, although, come to think of it, it could always be arranged, you know, I'll just er, I'll just get the BBC to sanction it obviously! But er, Frank, thank you very much for the time being

(dumb enough to spend your time typing out endless state-ments)

you are teaching one of your classes with something I wrote – generally I have to influence the youth of America one at a time and it involves a lot of time-consuming skulking and prowling • you are having trouble understanding what they told you to do • you are brown-nosing in SLC or Provo • you are working with idiots • you are someone who enjoys using buggy software to access filtered, mass-market content viewed through a confusing and offensively harsh Las Vegas-style aesthetic; you'll probably be concerned by this news • you are sooooo coming to this show with me • you are no longer welcome here • you are sending something insured, or when someone has overpaid you for an item as I did • you are set on giving me negative feedback should I give you negative feedback • you are still sitting here thinking about it, he's got you focusing on this negative energy • you are the praying type, regardless of religious affiliation or lack thereof, please find it in your heart to send your positive energies to my grandma, Rivka Bas Zlata, who's more than a tad under the weather and I'm freaking out about it • you are now one of the few, the proud, the aimlessly practicing in hopes of better wars to come • you are reading between the lines

(the owner of the secret decoder ring and as such have a right to be president of the club)

you are all enjoying the dinner and accommodations! If you are, then I want you to know that I selected this restaurant, typed the program, set-up the tables, cooked your dinner and Lou Hansen will be doing the dishes ... however, if you're not happy with the arrangements, then Lou is responsible for it all and I just happen to be here • you are often not sure who's the stuffed turkey • you are perfect just the way you are • you are never quite sure about what's going to happen next • you are bored, go to Mexico • you are thinking of buying one for the neighbourhood • you are definitely in trouble as you can get silicosis which will destroy your lungs • you are a little crazy about your friend Jan • you are helping with our plan to heal the earth and inhabit the galaxy • you are a hunter of fossils; earth science; kindergarten through sixth grade • you are an easy mark for some sleazy, opportunity-seeking pickpocket • you are not anti-Catholic post a link to comments by Ian Paisley, who is still fighting the Thirty Years War • you are using equipment that may belong to someone else • you are actually free to wear the suit anytime you like; you are not limited to wearing the suit at ham radio functions or emergency mobilizations • you are ready to go • you are sent to federal prison under Project Exile, prison rape will be an expected part of your future • you are unaware of it, last week Microsoft stepped up its anti-Linux FUD (Fear, Uncertainty and Doubt) campaign • you are a cop, talk this over with your brother officers – and with your union representatives – immediately • you are committing yourself to opening that trunk? "What will people think about the cold, unbending tools you are threatening that poor, innocent tire with? Where's the love in that tire iron? Where's the warmth in that, Jack? Can't we use kinder, gentler tools? You're going to get your hands dirty – and make us look bad doing it!" All of this is noise, of course, and irrelevant

(some clever electronic banking maneuver)*

you are way ahead of the pack • you are in like Flynn • you are
going to hand out • you are laughing • you are one of the best at
what you do and no one needs to tell you that • you are supposed
to play the story straight, whatever the facts are, and we're doing
that • you are a victim • you are sure you understand everything
you've been told • you are not sure which of these agencies is the
right one • you are enclosing payment • you are wrongly arrested
again • you are wrong • you are unemployed and plan to look for
a job within 60 days; you are on welfare • you are dealing with a
legitimate organization • you are finished • you are unsure about
anything • you are too embarrassed to get out of it • you are being
pressured • you are feeling uncomfortable then you need to tell
these people flat out that you aren't interested and you want them
to go away • you are doing what you need to in order to protect
yourself • "you are going to succeed against them," he said • you
are just going to create more confusion • you are missing your
little pod • you are disappointed

(if you aren't you should be)

you are being bullied • you are more likely to say "Aw, how cute!
He destroyed my bathroom!" than to say "Die, furball!" – so here
are a few questions you can ask yourself before bringing the little
terror into your home • you are being bullied? What can you do
if you see someone else being bullied? Are you a bully? For more
information: what is bullying? Bullying is when someone keeps
doing or saying things to have power over another person … you
are being bullied? Coping with bullying can be difficult, but
remember, you are not the problem, the bully is • you are saying
that bullying is okay with you • you are sometimes a bully, try to
find other ways to make yourself feel good • you are different in
some way, be proud of it! • you are too similar, but that's another
matter entirely

(misspelled in a grade six spelling bee by a kid who will eventually serve eight years in jail for manslaughter)

you are: a |_| reproachful look |_| college dropout |_| slimy little prick |_| proud of your work for dad's company |_| not the favourite child |_| first confrontation with a clown |_| punished for telling the truth |_| toilet overflowing |_| forced to kiss warty old relatives |_| forced to wear hand-me-downs |_| forced to perform in front of parents' friends |_| being put to bed when not sleepy |_| parents driving too slowly |_| receiving underwear for your birthday |_| scratchy new sweater |_| boring vacation |_| being family scapegoat |_| mom reading your secret diary |_| throwing up at school |_| insufferable brother |_| insufferable sister |_| being told to say "thank you" for the 10,000th time |_| being told to clean your room for the 100,000th time |_| cleaning your room |_| Republican parents |_| forced to wear totally stupid clothes |_| favourite TV show cancelled |_| dreaming about having no clothes at school |_| cleaning out cat box |_| parents calling you embarrassing nickname in front of friends |_| wetting your pants at school |_| being tattled on |_| tattling on someone and having it backfire |_| forced to eat spinach |_| forced to eat broccoli |_| parents threatening to send you to military school |_| military school |_| summer school |_| school |_| sunday school |_| dancing school |_| early bedtime strictly enforced |_| not getting dessert because you didn't eat your vegetables |_| grounded |_| allowance cut off |_| being told not to eat so fast |_| being told not to chew with your mouth open |_| being told to sit up straight |_| homework |_| socks as presents |_| handkerchief for birthday |_| parents telling you what you will be when you grow up |_| listening to parents fight in the next room |_| listening to parents fight in the same room |_| being hit by a parent |_| being kicked by a parent |_| slapped by a parent |_| spanked by a parent |_| beaten by a parent |_| burned by a parent |_| locked in closet |_| tortured |_| sexually molested |_| getting lost |_| being called "bad" |_| being called "lazy" |_| being called "selfish" |_| making your mom cry |_| meeting another kid with your name |_| being told "you are just not trying" |_| being forced to apologize when you don't mean it |_| not being allowed to go to a slumber party |_| being told "i know you could do better" |_| first time seeing dead dog in the road |_| first starving child seen on TV |_| first assassination seen on TV |_| first realization that death is permanent |_| first realization that death is inevitable |_| first realization that applies to you too |_| first ghost seen |_| being treated like a baby in front of friends |_| being chosen last for the team |_| not being invited to a birthday party |_| first bee sting |_| first booster shot |_| being forbidden to play with bad kids |_| fear of dogs |_| fear of vampires |_| fear of robots |_| fear of aliens |_| fear of sharks |_| fear of monsters |_| fear of bears |_| fear of lions |_| fear of psychopaths |_| fear of nuclear war |_| fear of dad |_| caught shoplifting |_| being told "you ought to be ashamed of yourself" |_| _____ [fill in the blank] |_| ongoing nameless dread

***

(better than bad, you're good)*

you are a newcomer with a theatrically hypersensitive soul and delusions of entitlement • you are smart enough to pose this question, you are smart enough to RTFM • you are unlikely to be the first person to notice an obvious deficiency; it is rather more likely that you are utterly clueless • you are bored • you are thinking • you are not working on everything else • you are too • you are working on the biggest things you could be working on, then you are Type-B procrastinating, no matter how much you are getting done • you are falling through the centre of the Earth, where would you end up?

(a quote within a quote desperately trying to escape)

you are right in the shadow of the radio towers, which could be creepy • you are probably unaware that there is no evidence for the existence of gods or goddesses – leave alone your master's particular pantheon • you are somehow different than the rest, totally oblivious to the ranting lunatic shrill screech that you all eventually become when occult, superstitious wishful thinking isn't enough to get reasoning, educated men and women to believe nonsense • you are desperately looking for a way to escape your misery • you are a mile away • you are already walking on thin ice, you might as well dance • you are in need • you are using and it won't let you experience the full wonder • you are weird, scary, freaky and on top of all that, once got held hostage by armed chimpanzees in Morocco • you are completely and utterly bored with nothing better to occupy yourself, you could watch the photos change over the next week and then • you are desperately keen to have a chance to comment • you are desperate to know the true story behind my unheralded disappearance from the cut-and-thrust world of blogging • you are not convinced • you are probably experiencing for yourself right about – er, um – now • you are overcome with an insane urge to read through the entire weekly archives from start to finish • you are – > • you are worried about Carly • you are nervous and right now, you're guzzling it like there's no tomorrow • you are two miles away • you are the weekly comic strip by Brad Yung, stay as you are • "you are cheering for Italy, right ?" "No, Korea," she replied • you are number 8 • "you are not gonna get paid, either one of you! Come on, let's go! Let's box!" – Raul Caiz, Jr • you are not convinced after reading that • you are a geek? Okay, show me the money • you are going to watch the spots • you are number 8 is now at: Magpie Magazines, Pulpfiction, ABC Book & Comic Emporium, Zulu Records, Scratch Records and the Comic Shoppe • you are an immigrant and not a foreigner • you are reading this – get better friends • you are truly evil if you are number 8

(a most noble swain)*

you are going to sell the idea that there was something besides oil that drew the Bush regime into a quagmire in Iraq, you might better take up selling bridges you don't own • you are also likely to stumble across the familiar names of Faraday, Karl Marx, George Eliot, Radclyffe Hall, Carl Rosa and Sir Ralph Richardson • you are saying things that are obvious to anyone who thinks honestly about the situation • you are retired, as if you were a feasted one and not the hostess of the meeting: pray you, bid these unknown friends to welcome; for it is a way to make us better friends, more known • you are not alone • you are lord of all the land, do good again, forget me not • you are a prince without a peer I have no present which could please • you are ready to cut • you are ready to applique • you are suitably close and any audience member is a viable target

(in absentia)

you are by no means a "stalker" • you are definitely overreacting
to surprise "hello"s so I'm really sorry • you are not planning on
using it? Posted by: xyng on June 11, 2002 02:54 pm Oh yeah
sorry about that, just wanted to know I got the right Dawn – but
I saw you at the study in Britain Fair with this other girl quite a
while ago and it's been hookup all the way if I got the wrong
person probably because I saw the wrong photo then excuse me
– silly grin – ooops Jeanette • you are right, she is amazing • you
are here • you are getting into it over your head • you are crying
because the one is so far away or whining because he or she won't
give you your space, the challenges of keeping love alive will be
many and mighty during your first year here at Yale • you are at it,
get a room • you are a light • you are too strong for – blink • you
are not • you are so beautiful when you sleep • you are new, but I
know who you are • you are going to fool me

(engaging in self nullifying behaviour)

you are ferreting with floss, who might have a bit of polecat in her, vicious, but knows how to work a warren, hearing this the lad doesn't feel quite so good about seeing rabbits scuttling into hedge bottoms on his morning jog, so the thing is, all told, the jogging making the lad otter, the lack of drink is no bad thing, but it still don't stop that black sick coming up from time to time, he real worried about this, but can't face no nosy receptionist, no patronizing doctor, but then one time round for a house meal, Tudor's spot, all his friends there or good acquaintants, either way there's a bit of east European wine going round along with food, a bit of Tokay, if it's spelt that way or even if not, some Hungarian bull's blood and the subject of the story, takes nothing more than a glass and before the worst course of carp in sour cream is done he's writhing on the floor, stomach heaving, thin trickle of blood wetting his lips, they panic then, no time for any doctor, it's nine-nine-nine not that the lad realizes as he passes out way afore the ambulance arrives, leaving Anastasia feeling bad about that meal, she putting a lot of effort into everything she's cooking, couple of courses, endless appetizers and it's ruined, she don't want to think this way, she wants to be all concerned, specially when Dai was there too, recently moving into the house Dai's your man's brother, not that blood relationships ought to have too much to bear on such matters, but sometimes it helps a little to know something of the background, so that in the end if a conclusion is reached, it is one that is contingent upon some sort of relationship between assertion and circumstance, but then, suppose none of this is really on your mind at the moment, suppose what is really wanting knowing is what happened to the gaje whisked off to hospital, but the problem is that truth is duller than action – orst ooe, so little really happens it just like that, this spray of dots, just going to feel a scratch on your hand, then I'm going to inject you with an anaesthetic, you might feel your hand go cold, what I want you to do is to start counting up to 10: one twothreefour, in recovery, hurting to hell, disorientated and you no longer possess both legs to stand upon or your ingrowing toenails have been semi-sorted or that rudimentary stomach of the appendix has been separated from you, all you can say to folks back on the ward is don't make me laugh, cliché but none the less worthy of being stated, but the dot-dot-dot that is being talked about here is something slightly different, so okay the lad blacks out, but upon waking, there he is all clinical white, tucked up in bed wearing a paper-dressing gown and no one seems to know why, the notes by the bed are occasionally tutted over, he is told that he may go to the toilet by himself and if he needs anything to ring the bell, but bugger all else seems to be happening, save come the nighttime, when Tudor, Anastasia, Dai, Keith, Dave and his last year's girlfriend decide to shew, given the state of the syntax, that poor saddo don't know if the girlfriend's Dave's or his own, he's beginning to get confused, though not as bad as the end, when the waking dreams came for him, but even calling them that is saying too much and not a little judgmental, but

(a sense of alienation)

you are keenly aware they are not capable of feeling what you are feeling or knowing what you are going through • you are suffering or how you cry out and pray deep into each midnight • you are spiritually bankrupt • you are going through the dark night – they probably do not even know what it is • you are profoundly aware of the suffering of humanity and the cruelty of one person to another • you are not given access, number two you fear, number three you are not culturally comfortable – so these are the factors which finally go into making what you call ghettoization and I'd call clustering together for a sense of security • you are depressed, your makeup will be on straight and you'll be well-dressed • you are having a conversation, saying things like "Oh, doesn't she look nice!" or "That's a pretty dress," and inside you are having all these images of doom and despair • you are eating and it doesn't taste like anything, it tastes like straw and you say "How delicious!" add to a personal sense of failure and futility the actual or implied message, from others, that it's your fault and the sense grows even greater • you are on your own, Chiron

(a dentist, you take delight in causing great pain)

you are easily offended, here is the disclaimer to stop reading now
• you are in South America and you want to telephone someone
in Russia, perhaps in Siberia • you are looking at the colours of a
person's aura • you are advised to go back and re-read the previous
lessons, for in this lesson and lesson nine we are going to prepare
the ground for leaving the body • you are clear about the nature
of the molecular structure of the body – you may run into some
difficulties • you are afraid it will hurt; you sit there in the chair in
fear • you are afraid that you are going to faint with the shock, so
you feed the fear • you are sitting in a completely dark room at the
top of a skyscraper; before you there is a large picture window
panoramavindu covered by a black blind *rullegardin*, a blind
which has no pattern, nothing which could prove a distraction •
you are able to control your thoughts as do the adepts and the
masters • you are inside a big rubber balloon, pushing, pushing •
you are accustomed to idling drive-about in a room – you cannot
safely venture outside • you are journeying to freedom; it is only
when back in the body that you need to feel imprisoned, encased
in clay, weighted down by a heavy body which does not respond
very well to spiritual commands • you are lying flat on your back
on a bed • you are falling asleep; that was the astral swaying • you
are not afraid, if you do not twitch, the astral body will slowly float
off, it will just drift away to the end or the side of the bed where
quite gently, without any shock whatsoever, it will gradually sink
so that the feet touch, or almost touch the floor • you are well
acquainted, perhaps a close relative who lives in a neighbouring
city • you are astral travelling – the body relays a warning and you
are "reeled in" with the speed of thought • you are in the astral
stage consciously, you will see colours more brilliantly than you
do in the flesh • you are in the astral and you want to return to the
physical, you should keep calm, you should let yourself think of
the flesh body, think that you are going to go back and that you
are going to get in • you are there, drifting, undulating slightly, just

as when you left the body • you are stiff • you are afraid of them •
you are afraid • you are alone, of course – at midday and again in
the afternoon – and again before you retire and go to sleep • you
are disturbed or distressed during the proposed day • you are
forcing another body out of yourself, imagine that the ghostly
form of the astral is being pushed out • you are standing there
looking at your physical component and wondering what to do
next • you are nothing like you expected • you are being com – 52
Object Wershler-Henry and Kennedy page 5 pletely irrational •
you are a self-consum – 53 *Object* Wershler-Henry and Kennedy
page 6 – ing artifact

(the kind of apathy that can only be generated by the spoken word debate)

you are all a little bit more informed • you are greatly mistaken in considering that we now have something fundamentally different • you are not gonna say what you really think? • you are publishing too many comments that are both well informed and justifiably dismissive of your conservative "family values" approach • you are interested in the fuzzy sociology of communications and struc-tures, then imagine your own 15-year-old daughter at a sewing machine for 80 hours a week at 10 p an hour living in a bunker away from her family and consider the societal implications of that • you are brought up completely oblivious to the fact that there was a civil war after WWII • you are going to train people, train the ones who are going to do something with it! • you are going to vote Liberal if Labour has no policies – and do they? All the donkeys who claim to be worse off under Libs won't have any joy under Labour • you are so staunchly Labour • you are either a fool or a liar, Mr. Roberts! Which is it? All this from a jerk-off journal that has been bemoaning and bewailing the taking to task of a rampaging gang of fag church-terrorists by the Catholic Archbishop of Melbourne George Pell a week or so ago • you are talking about art and I'm talking about cultural policy and they are quite different things • you are a Wagner or a Yeats nowadays, so really what we have here is a state society, deciding a broad agenda of pluralism • you are saying that the idea of corporate money being dirty is, I agree, slightly dangerous, in that we should look at the people who actually choose the exhibitions and go back from that to government policy • you are asking really is that public funding for culture is trying to sort out what • you are on the right track in terms of the book, because the book is about whether or not art should be judged as art or whether it should be judged as social policy • you are not saying that at all • you are right, I should have remembered her famous article "Why I Do Not Call Myself A Feminist" • you are living or working abroad, but why did you choose not to live there and have data at your fingertips? I'm not being critical of either choice, by the way • you are attracted to and care about me • you are either from that region or are one of the scholars of that time period • you are doing a great disservice to women in general by confining your whole attention to sexism • you are right, it's so terrible really – the trivial preoccupations of the educated elite are the root of much that is wrong

(an unimportant stanza in an unimportant Bob Southey epic)*

you are old, Father William, the young man said • you are
prepared to follow the rules (1) everyone entering will have only
one set of votes no matter how many poems they enter (2) you
will be sent an IM once the contest has closed asking you to vote
for your top three poems (3) I will allocate points as such first
place will receive 4 points second 2 points third 1 point the poem
with the most accumulated points wins (4) only poets entering
can vote but may not vote for themselves (5) result will be
announced 48 hrs after I send out IMs asking for the votes or
sooner if all votes are in (6) any poet not voting, will have any
votes cast for them handed to top three places • you are right
about him • you are my friend, yet I've begun to doubt if what you
say is true • you are my friend, and will support my fight against
the plights of life, yet as you guard my back you stab me with your
knife • you are atheist, many poets, friends, try to shove their
morals and beliefs down my throat and I hate it, so I won't do the
same to you • you are doing well • you are already a member • you
are just friends • you are great!!!! Melanie – reply? • you are in the
21st century and I suggest you go read an anthology • you are "the
best of cut-throats" • you are a beaten man at war with the dictates
of his heart • you are all powerless and to make me choose
between a suicide and a murder? – Jean-Paul Sartre 1905–1980,
French novelist, dramatist, philosopher, political activist • you are
asleep • you are always recovering • you are perhaps not lying, but
you are not telling the truth • you are absolutely sure I'll never find
out the truth • you are always recovering • you are expecting the
reader to struggle? You use too many abstractions

(the neurochemical dopamine during a bout of particularly raunchy sex with a not-quite-loved one)*

you are on the conservative side, this book is not for you • you are looking at the definition of booty call, friends with benefits, hookup, no strings attached, etc. • you are plain lazy • you are playing Southampton, I will be there! Also, I am really loving the T-shirts! mwah! mwah! xxx • you are having fun, it's love • you are rewarded, you feel good • you are playing the guild, the "other side," your buddies, etc. • you are here: BBC > Science & Nature > Hot Topics > Science Of Love • you are a thrill-seeker or do you prefer your pipe and slippers? • you are not a stalker are you? You're not the type who checks her messages five times a day, will call me in the middle of the night are you? Will I be safe around you? When screening a girl, you establish that you are the chooser and that she is the chaser • you are not like all the other girls • you are pretty, but what else have you got going for you? • you are regarded as the class nerd – a total dork and everyone makes fun of you • you are a 9 • you are on the same wavelength with a guy • you are affecting your relationship, even if your partner hasn't caught on to what's happening • you are a free agent, and your crush is the one dividing his affections • you are involved in an emotional affair – and not just a healthy friendship • you are having an emotional affair, and they'll nod in sympathy • you are not having sex so it's not cheating, is it?

(an instance of pre-emptory teleology)*

you are incorrect • you are making a categorical error • you are
going to posit natural causes and talk reason: wonderful • you
are going to talk faith, just admit it and be honest about it • you are
agreeing with the front-loaders, but I could be confused • you
are correct • you are assuming that either everything is a miracle
or everything is science, without understanding that if miracles
occur, then there is necessarily an interplay • you are right; it is too
general to function as usable advice • you are concerned with –
and I agree, it's an important concern – then traditional liberal
ways of thinking will be of more service than Foucauldian ones •
you don't know what he meant • you are going to quote it anyway

(living in a post-theory, post-language writing, post-sound poetry, post-literate age, so let's stop writing crap)*

you are singing gibberish • you are into the poet's society of boring • you are really any good, that is • you are just as bad, if not worse, then me let me know • you are an insufferable know-it-all who doesn't know anything at all • you are being a bit judgmental though, in this poem • you are thwarted because of your lack of interest in the subject, Daniel, and then later on it seems you are angry with someone for no particularly good reason • you are in a stupid frame of mind • you are him and you are reading him • you are stuck in the middle of the end you'll never know where you are because you are not quite by the middle and the end's not very far if the middle of the end is the middle if you can't find your way out of the middle

(a reference to the small font size of this poem)*

you are going round in circles describing how your poetry embodies your true self that people often overlook • you are abusing it • you are trying to exit their wretched hive of scum and villainy as rapidly as you can find the back button • you are the 2,317th visitor to this page • you are not comfortable publishing in a magazine that leans heavily toward political poetry, then don't waste your time and ours • you are looking for everything in its range that may fit the description • you are not in it – that's it • you are belittling me • you are not turned on by my bejewelled beret? I bethink not! Shall I play for you some bebop? • you are around just the right people, people of a certain age, people with a certain countercultural appreciation, those words will resonate and someone will respond: "No, man" • you are putting on airs • you are thinking, what a great name, I wonder what it means • you are smart, funny… no, no, it's not that • you are going with this • you are satisfied! Have a specific question? Get answers here! Ask us a specific question and get a personalized answer from a qualified member! • you are satisfied! • you are guaranteeing that those pages will get an inside view of some editor's garbage can • you are in the same boat as everybody else • you are poor like we are; stand in a bookstore, read the journal, and put it back on the shelf when you are done

(going to sell out the first chance you get)

you are number 1 • you are still screwed • you are standing in line,
you or someone else should be dialling the charge-by-phone
number the minute the tickets go on sale • you are not first in line
• you are on hold, you hang up • you are paying long distance
charges • you are going the phone route, you need to research this
in advance • you are out of luck • you are on a modem, you won't
stand a chance • you are at a show ticketless, or with a sucky seat,
you should plan on hitting the venue box office the minute it
opens the day of the show and keep returning periodically • you
are outside the venue pounding the pavement, looking for a
ticket, it becomes a waiting game • you are patient • you are looking
to buy by the pallet, you can come and pick out your pallets, or
they can be shipped from our warehouse – remember though,
since each pallet is different, it would be impossible to ever have
an accurate list or catalogue • you are staring at your $300 hard-
earned bucks worth of crummy literature and wonder how you
are going to do the same trick • you are saying and doesn't stop to
ask, you are sunk • you are all wrong here, it's worth much more
• you are actually going to raise your hand • you are sure it's in
good shape, that's not a bad price • you are getting started, let
someone else make the first bid • you are still expected to pay for
the merchandise before you leave

(yawning stop it!)

you are under 18 we can't let you join • you are over the age of consent you can hop on over • you are under 18 and can't join, well then, we're afraid you can't check out our archives either • you are really conservative and get freaked out simply by innocent conversations about homosexual relationships • you are so sheltered, man • you are a late bloomer so I'll let it slide • you are dating them or something • you are bisexual, man • you are right • you are better than a soap opera • you are getting rid of carbon dioxide • you are holidaying in Iceland with two friends, staying with another friend in central Reykjavik • you are talking to some people back home, the others are watching TV and everyone's thinking of getting to bed – it's been a long day • you are shivering in the cold night air • you are staying with has already said he doesn't usually notice these displays, much to everyone's disbelief • you are left with nothing but clear skies

(a persnickety line whose potential offensiveness is enhanced by its referential obscurity)*

you are just a sincere person trying to get through to me! What went wrong? First of all, it may not be your fault • you are in the hot dog case, be sure to check the weight of your package • you are willing to accept the Ford 500 as a "cuv"? Looks like a car to me, but it fits your definition • you are able to find nothing • you are making things too complicated • you are doing it to earn a living so who cares • you are feeding yourselves and paying your mortgage with income from showing it • you are putting Heather's writing second • you are able to do that • you are seeing the old masthead, that is a cache issue • you are asking for donations, but at the same time focusing on advertising – it just seems wrong in some way • you are golden • you are going to continue • you are not giving up on this thing • you are too! • you are out of arguments so baiting is all you have left (all out to get me damn you)[†]

you are not a bad-ass • you are at that moment, but almost instantly you're in a new place, as soon as it's recorded, so it's just basically a window into where you're going in the future • you are supposed to announce that today is your religion's daylight savings holiday • you are easily offended, gullible or don't have a sense of humour • you are waiting, please take our first-ever Quizilla user poll • you are famous • you are too • you are good, we give you money, you are a dick, you are faded • you are going to sin • you are going to sin against God, not the bureaucracy • you are going to Hell • you are going to Hell for your "moral bankruptcy" • you are lucky enough to have in your possession a "get out of jail free" card • you are in big trouble and, according to certain humourless readers, the ultimate in "trouble" is Hell! But you just slap down a card and waltz merrily away, leaving your opponent befuddled • you are not convinced

(mixing memory with desire)

you are number one you are always having fun who's got the
bomb so put away your guns and put away your bombs clap your
hands and sing Happy Mondays we're not as big as we feel well it
pained the first time the smell of your breath creating a taste that
still lingers in my mouth longing for the hollowed feeling you left
with me when you left from me my memory serves me too well
we're not as big as we feel obviously better off without you I try
to sound profound I've found I'm definitely no pro masochistic
reminiscing of what I've been missing it's so hard to finally let go
we're not as big as we feel heartache take me away you'd sit
patiently while I'd experiment with what my voice can actually do
I'd add some lyrics about you Andy I love Andy! Are you listening?
Ah hell you never listen to me we're not as big as we feel chorus
losing sleep we have a good thing an understanding how together
we'd give 'em hell but now I'm hearing things a plot against me
and a dear friend since we were 15 hanging and playing around
we had an offering to make a better friend a pick that says how
long could spark another song and strum a memory I'm all alone
I'm losing sleep so help me out and if you've got a friend like
James Taylor said and sung about and when the truth rolled in
with the tide two heavy colours rose off my shoulders and lit the
sky but now darkness casts on opposing sides we will get by we
will get by out of love chorus oh my God oh my God you are just
a wolf in sheepskin oh my God my mother was always right
clichés becoming the universal truth dark Monday theatres thank
you John Wilkes Booth oh my God I'm singing out of context oh
my God the scenery is to blame this guitar like a needle stuck in
my vein I need to grow up and get myself clean all the party kids
trying to make a scene cliquey scene trying to be the next new hot
teen sexy teen I don't know them I don't want to oh my God your
life's through rose-coloured glasses oh my God your thoughts all
choreographed Miss Gepetto's in charge of pulling the strings
priorities lost to ever-changing dreams if I could control my

thinking the first thing I'd do would be to stop thinking of you if I could control your feelings the first thing I'd do would be to make you feel like I do chorus down again yeah I don't know exactly it was way back when things were a whole lot greener then but today I just don't know what to believe in it's impossible to find love these days I spend 'em sitting around the house just feeling sorry for myself maybe I should get over you back before love got lazy back then nothing could phase me but today everything's so crazy chorus I don't have time for anyone that don't have time for me and it was from you that I learned this philosophy and to love you I paid mentally love was shot down in flames my story's a tragedy and the worst part of it all it was my friend holding me down again no it shouldn't feel this way love is not supposed to hurt it should set you free but every now and then you come around and say you are my friend tell me you love me again well it's a good thing I know you'd fake life to get what you want by telling lies and it makes you high to see me low I've had to watch your self-confidence grow every time that you pull your love away throw all your happiness in my face fireworks without a doubt baby you and me could help this love team out it seems odd though I do agree if we could work things out the first time I saw you fireworks brown sweatered shirts tan stripes nice style you've got that kind of smile that makes me smile the first time I saw you fire looking forward up all night figuring out me and you do things that make me laugh new and exciting things another chance to if I could hold you it's funny how things tend to work out and I'm looking forward again it's been it's been tough for both of us but before long we won't be lonely again feelings last over night in hopes that three longs years might bring a chance to if I could hold you if we put our hands together wouldn't you feel so much better if we put our hearts together wouldn't you feel love more than ever more than ever it's funny how things tend to work out and I'm looking forward again we're waking up kings car cyclical vacations where we covered all the nation we're in for a long summer drive with stolen verbal melodies sadness flows through burnt Christmas trees in times like these where we have been waiting so long with Jim Jeff and Andy we'll set boys' and girls' bodies in motion and with lines like these you should be singing along well it's driving us crazy how they don't know rock and roll a boy and a boy together create four-way friendships lifelong teammates never saw Florida flamingoes hey prospector we danced our final flamenco sadness flows through veins vodka veins we could go play on a Saturday Dairy Queen Sundays Peanut Buster Parfaits okay you make it look easy you make it look so Goddamn easy chorus loop waiting for you to smile call and make things better but could you even care your words hurt untrue not a nice thing to do when someone's got a crush on you well I guess now I know what you are about instead of hanging you are flaking out just feeling me fade out and even though it's still hard to watch you go but before I'd like to let you know that someone's got someone's got a crush on you oh my God from Mount Everest to the Everglades re-obtaining doesn't mean it's found she's the cruellest month of all oh my God a girl who's like the calendar she's changing almost every day sooner or later so predictable yet the holidays land on the different days every year thought loses shape I've lost my touch missing time with you thinking how my favourite colour is fast becoming sugar fast becoming you borders sorry for when I was gone I'll buy you diamond jewellry to make up for the time everything in the world is you and you are everything to me we used to have a good rapport with each other and everything was painted beautiful red in colour including our love it hurts sometimes to think how much I was wrong and how much you were right arguing was a waste of words and I wish I could hear your words again I swear to good you're God at this we talked until our faces turned blue until our mouths just moved and our ears no longer had to work

I'm so glad you came that's why I try anymore luckily nothing left was unsaid so we shared a bed both now with embarrassed red his busy hands led to his dizzy head led to his heart's so woozy and even if he's a genius would you act like him arrogant he belongs in the movies his lips on the silver screen aw man fuck it let the radio play kept still talking until we lost our voices feel now that I'm educated still no intelligentleman I'm so glad you came that's why I try anymore chorus the things we said not listening to those lies you can't explain well I can play those games too and so I'm sending them right back to where they came from where they came with the pictures the lies and the promises that you left written down as proof to date those past words I'd hear you say to put me through this after feeling the same strain could somehow make you happier it seems difficult to explain and I go through all this before you wake so I can be happier and to feel safe from you of all the problems I've had this one's still going out or still coming up and on a doubt a late shout to call about could fix the good gone bad and all those good friends I have it feels great to feel love like that but there's only one two three chances charmed before you feel like a wreck and the blue sky warms your neck chorus whales of the desert hop on now and ride the fame of a wave we can buy crowns and act like kings we're the whales of the desert but there's no TV cameras in the desert oh no one fish in a bowl is the biggest and smallest of all we'll try to make it after the fall we'll try to make it springtime

(sitting with a soggy ass at some reading in High Park really wishing
you were somewhere else)

you are one of us

(a portable Greek reader that is going to party like it's 1999)

you are still likely to go see it in the cinema for the full cinematic experience • you are probably going to go out and buy it on video or DVD anyway • you are mistaken for the other institution/ brand • you are okay • you are informed you will behave responsibly and cease to encourage my son's participation with your magazine in any way • you are swimming through an awkward party moment, against seemingly unforgiving swales, when for example you want to escape the conversational persistence of a particularly desperate guest, don't just lunge for the nearest lawyer at the party and make introductions • you are not my servant, I am yours • you are happy now that you have had your way • you are tired of feeling like a prisoner on Sunday afternoon, tired of the futility of another series of downs ending in three and out, tired of having your hopes inflated by New Jersey "journalists" only to watch them go up in flames as another Hindenberg of a season crashes down • you are great fun • you are not Michiko – conversely I am not her • you are excited and I'll send you a Swatch plastic-strapped, working interior: happy 14th birthday! • you are not alone • you are right, it is • you are stuck gurgling at your computer, but I'm gonna keep fuckin your mind like the film of Zapruder • you are seeing around the traps • you are not supposed to use mimesis • you are not supposed to kill your mother and father, you are not supposed to imitate anything • you are from another world, not this one? That you are someone else, not the person you are supposed to be? That must be the way it feels to be Jewish and even if you think you are not a Jew, if you've ever felt that way you may be Jewish too

(going on with your doggy life)

you are an angel and will continue to watch over us • you are with
your lifelong friend Chappi and together you wait for us, both of
you young and healthy once again • you are at peace • you are okay,
that you are healthy and happy although far away • you are gone
from our home but will forever live in our hearts • you are awake
all night with cramps in your legs and you won't move them • you
are and what you are going to do to them • you are going to have
to use it • you are going to spend a lot of time talking about yourself
• you are going to have to be arrested for manslaughter, drug or
firearm possession, public indecency, wearing an outfit that
clashes, or assault • you are all that, although threatening that you
can kick the ass of anyone who would argue this point even if you
are a big sissy is usually enough to back your claims • you are
thinking: "I can't sing about homo lovin' and be accepted by the
mainstream, breeding audience" • you are wrong • "you are in a
vehicle going the speed of light – what happens if you turn on the
headlights?" • you are it • you are still an idiot • you are completely
clueless • you are bi unless you are just getting married for health
insurance or to make mom and pop happy • you are about to
engage in the deed, my suggestion is to get her on her hands and
knees, then "subtly" make your intentions known by casually
knockin' on the back door • you are off target, then sorry pal,
you've been waved off • you are small • you are not too big and if
you have access to a row of lockers • you are Davy Crockett,
however • you are like me and haven't even thought about making
a list, better yet gotten around to checking it twice, here are a few
gift suggestions which may help ensure that you and your family
don't end up on the Fox Network's Christmas special, *America's
Best Holiday Massacres Caught On Tape* • you are actually going
to leave him a tip for ringing up that breakfast big bite and the
large peanut butter and jelly Slurpee • you are required by law to
eat everything that's set out on the table • you are like most of us,
you look for a mate who's compatible, who you want to spend

207

your life with and who will put up with your counting peoples'
toes to make sure they have five on each foot • you are President
Clinton, you look for someone who will stand by you even when
you repeatedly show incredibly bad taste in your choice of
liaisons • you are Elizabeth Taylor or Mickey Rooney, you pretty
much just look for anyone you haven't married yet

(the interplay between the quotidian and the extraordinary)

you are all aware by now I am very much out of my depth • you are her friend and I wanted you not to hear it from anywhere else • you are quite like him, you know – more conservative, but more thoughtful – it's a potent combination • you are only going to play bank • you are responsible for yourself and you'd better shape up • you are as unilateralist as we are • you are experiencing population decline • you are allowed and maybe even expected to kill family members, it will become ever more difficult to distinguish between murder and suicide • you are implicitly referring to these immigrants as "maggots," you've slipped over the edge into a frightening form of race-baiting • you are an equal opportunity employer, provided the party is equally enthusiastic about your understanding of Dante's understanding of Beatrice • you are going to step on toes somewhere • you are in this spectrum of debate? PG: Well, I think having said that we take that part of Lyotard saying that reading Kant is essential, especially the *Third Critique*, it's important to point out that it is the *First Critique* that has dominated in this part of the world • you are saying is that you should leave that to the specialist • you are supposed to support, support this fellow and so on • you are experiencing her artwork, if you want • you are interested in it because it has something to offer you in terms of your own project • you are not bringing high-culture into this • you are not distinguishing high-culture from low-culture? PG: If you look at high-culture and how it has developed, I'm imagining this now, maybe you could say, that some high-culture actually developed out of low-culture by sort of having this element of the absolute in it • you are rewarded for knowing what your fellow citizens are likely to say their delusions are • you are pouring silt-whip over that old New England Cherry Cobbler • you are driven from the country which has sustained you for generations, I and I and I and I • you are tired of London, you are tired of life • you are at that stage of fitness and going into competition it's like a love affair … • you are relatively immune from discrimination of the sexist type • you are beating a clump of seaweed with a stick or rock or a shell • you are a woman • you are actually constructing a world, the thing itself, rather than an image of it and I'm told that in the outer reaches of physics and cosmology this is no simple question – that, as among the Pythagoreans, the figures by their logical inevitability announce their necessary being not as ancillary but as constitutive elements • you are always trying to keep up midway between the poles • you are holding time's cutting edge in your right hand ride cymbal, a simultaneity of holding and shaping • you are going to be able to write rules for this sort of case? I really need to see your rules! • you are seeing, rather than a subjective view of perception what you believe you are seeing • you are gone • you are not, but I'm taking you in for questioning, which is different

(a ravenous carnivore who lusts after the feeling of animal blood
tracing the crevasses of your chin)*

you are assuming I live a life of hedonism and rampant immorality
• you are Jesus's personal spokesperson, or you are being a wee bit
judgmental • you are a Catholic and believe in the three-in-one-
person, that's a heretical view in itself • you are an Israelite of old
• you are no longer allowed to be God's favoured servant • you are
famished • you are in Heaven rather than just north • you are having
a party • you are ready for the feast of a lifetime • you are interested,
these books will take you there quicker than a cattle drive • you
are ready • you are training heavily it is a necessity • you are gotten
me loving another depressing band, The Decemberists • you are
first on my list

(a captain's log, supplemental)

you are back home, on Vulcan • you are clear for takeoff runway
one five left • "you are angry when you are beautiful" • you are
compromising our productivity • you are staying for a while,
young man • you are nervous … otherwise you like it fine • you
are hereby ordered to stand down and prepare for boarding • you
are in grave danger • you are weaving a fabrication to me • "you
are here" Vessel: "Commander McBessy, at your service" • you are
somewhere in hyperspace • you are completely lost, there's a good
fellow • you are a good person • you are not • you are trespassing
in the happy fun dominion • you are near • you are very wrong!
Beverly comes proudly out, adorned in rich fabrics and gold and
jewels • you are back on the *Enterprise* • "you are sure," said
Lancelot, leaning on the rail by Gawain's station, "that it was
assimilating a sorcerer that's given the golem their time travel
capability?" "Must have been," said Nimue, popping upright
again • "you are certain you know what point in time to find the
golem sorcerer?" "Must be my own native time," Nimue said, as
on the screen she operated the cave controls, flipping switches
and turning cranks and working levers, "since it was this me, from
my now, that your signal drew into this now" • "you are sure," said
Riker, casually leaning on the rail by La Forge's station, "that it was
assimilating a Timelord that's given the Borg their time travel
capability?" "Must have been," said the Doctor, popping upright
again • "you are certain you know what point in time to find the
Borg Timelord?" "Must be my own native time," the Doctor said,
as on the screen he operated the Tardis controls, flipping switches
and turning cranks and working levers, "since it was this me, from
my now, that your signal drew into this now" • you are so eager to
reclaim your life on *Voyager*, Tom • you are near • you are waaay
wrong! [Beverly comes proudly out, adorned in rich fabrics and
gold and jewels] • you are back on the *Enterprise* • you are a friend
of mine, I have since bathed • you are fiercely loyal almost to a
fault • you are saying • you are in pain

(a metonymic slide)

you are off to a vague, dispiriting start • you are not gonna get
there if you keep missing your flights • you are being patient, but
at what point does Zeno's Paradox come into play and you figure
enough time has passed you by? Do you feel foolish for waiting
so long? Does your impatience, a fiery, passionate impulse that
seems more like life than the alternative, battle with received
wisdom and genteel guilt? Do you tell your heart to keep beating?
Or do you just ask it to keep beating when it decides to show you
who's boss? The adrenal impulses, the raw emotions, the reflexes
the flight-or-fight – aren't they reality? Aren't they the blue-collar
workers keeping your world safe and comfortable, appropriate
for a quiet night at home reading in the big chair? You have to
calm yourself down • you are nostalgic for the atmosphere,
Mount Nelson will fulfill your colonist fantasies out and about,
1998 • you are a new child of this land you will learn how to jump
like a kangaroo you will learn how to find your way in the bush
you will be told all of the myths and the legends the land will
embrace you warmly feeding you all the food from her body •
"you are from?" and the "Where you are at?" • "you are from"
signals the impossibility of complete integration – it is a question
which foregrounds "the bottomline of cultural identity" by
equating cultural identity with national identity • you are gonna
get a call to be in a Calvin Klein ad or anything • you are likely to
find • you are nowhere • you are interested, inquire 'cause we
should be able to get any of them • you are not already convinced,
or are over them already, or always found their vocals grating, or
for whatever reason aren't a fan • you are anything like our co-
worker Marc, then it's all about the amazing voice and certainly
not about the truly lame album cover • you are at all interested in
the possibilities of mind expansion through maximum riff-
bludgeonment over time and haven't scored this yet, do so! • you
are going to own just one "post-rock" record, this would be the
one to get • you are thinking how seriously kick-ass a song is, they

slip up and start sort-of-rapping or scratching or playing that weird sort of bouncy nu-metal and it makes me cringe • you are not a vinyl diehard, this CD is certainly recommended now • you are leaving a corpse? Pearl: Putting on gloves I knew you wouldn't be able to stand the thought of me being respectable again • you are walking out for the very same reason she did • you are the great has-been • you are supposed to know the lot • you are too old for it anymore

(a pipefitter with a penchant for Descartian ontology)*

you are having a clear and distinct perception right now, Walter! I have my manuscript right here, if I may quote: • you are a controversial figure; you engage in double-talk, delivering a gentle message in French and English and a radical – even extremist – one in Arabic • you are wondering how to get your own icon next to your comment • you are breathing oh, to hear your voice so near oh, to tremble in your laughter oh, to soak up all your tears oh • you are watching or planning on watching this series, you may hate that I'm revealing details • you are derived from hydrocarbons • you are just getting warmed up • you are more likely to find students drinking beer to MTV than a novel idea that may challenge the status quo • you are not having a hallucination? maybe Descartes was right that you are dreaming? • you are putting Descartes before the horse! • you are so hot why are you broke? asked the engineer • you are dependent on the working poor? Tricky • you are suffering from what the French call a *deformation professionnelle* • you are cursing at the camera because you want to override something • you are trying this while a musician is helping you get sounds by playing, and they have headphones on, you'll learn to do this test as fast as possible to avoid freaking them out or pissing them off • you are not with me • you are walking down the alley and you see the dumpster is not on fire? The mathematician puzzles over the question for awhile and he finally says "I light the dumpster on fire" • you are in the wrong class • you are smoking, but it must be pretty damn good • you are saying it is possible – just like Tyler has been patiently by the way I don't think I have the ability do what you've done here Tyler – and so calmly trying to tell you – everything you can possibly say is possible • you are a "brain in a vat" you are pretending to be someone you are not • you are pondering the idiocy of the question you just asked, then – yes • you are sayin'?! Did you say "Crosses the road?" How many have ya got? Peter, Paul and Mary • you are most motivated by: trying to take over the world! • you are afraid of others finding out that you are learning Dafa? Cultivation practice is a very serious matter • you are embarrassed to give it a correct position – this is human beings' true shame • you are wearing a new outfit that you are feeling very confident in • you are noticed • you are outside having a great time, you also need to be safe • you are a heterosexual male, but one time you used a feminine nick "just to mess with the horny net geeks" • you are too far gone! • you are broke and your modem burns out and you go out on to the streets to sell your body to get a new one • you are willing to risk a divorce because your husband doesn't like all the time you are spending on the computer • you are willing to sell a kidney to get to the next #anne-rice channel meet • you are risking your job by staying on #anne-rice in the afternoon from antha: • you are an *X-Files* fan and go on #x-files just to say "does anyone here like *The X-Files*?" • you are talking to them on the phone * you hack your server idle time "so lamers donut bug me" * you've ever actually used "donut" or "woii" in a sentence * your nick is mentioned on an irc web page or worse • you are telling someone about all your friends and it turns out they are all on IRC • you are reading this • you are addicted to IRC when you find stupid reasons to log into your shell account, knowing full well you can type "IRC" from there and be there in 2 seconds" from: norahs • you are away from a computer for more than a few hours • you are from the island of Malta • you are hiding under a chair and then actually go and do it • you are late for work • you are using the irc to conduct settlement conferences about your upcoming divorce • you are in a liberal arts college, but all of your friends understand "*lol*, brb, re, kewl" etc! You and your boyfriend/girlfriend broke up because he/she wouldn't

let you get online when you spent winter break at his/her house •
you are reading primary sources – any artifacts created in the
time period that you are studying • you are what you believe do
you ever wonder how some people can be cheerful and optimistic
most of the time, while others seem down and gloomy? Tell me:
Whose company do you prefer? Since I'm not a doctor, I have no
idea if personality is determined by genetics, environment or my
guess, both but what matters is since we spend so little time on
this planet, we must do what we can do enjoy our lives • you are
not eating a snack, if so, a thousand pardons or taking an insulin
shot, but since these health challenges are our reality, we have to
do what we can to make the best of things • you are feeling like
Grumpy Gus; I'm suggesting we find ways to circumvent the
problems we face with any diversion that holds appeal to you and
that will vary day-to-day • you are homebound? You know what
to do: rent a video and have your popcorn in privacy • you are
homebound, buy a beautiful art book to enjoy or borrow one
from the library • you are homebound, make a new friend on the
Internet • you are well aware, no matter what our plight, we're
alive and that's plenty to celebrate on its own • you are a fan of
Oprah Winfrey, you are most likely familiar with her stance on
the importance of gratitude in your life • you are, however, having
a particularly bad day and can't think of anything to be grateful
for, you can write something such as, "I'm glad today is over and
I can go to sleep" • you are interested, I can create an on-line grat-
itude journal so all of us can participate; otherwise, keep your
thoughts to yourself

(believing this crap they are feeding you)

you are known for will be lost in your age and unevolving spirits
awaken oh Moloch of parental forget of life liberty and their own
youth! Oh Moloch of I generation falling to this same shame! Oh
Moloch of all parents falling to this! Oh Moloch of my room with
no windows and walls growing higher! Oh Moloch of generational
quietude no more voice but multinational corporations and
money and shame and lust for more more more! You will be
shunned as your era will lose its aura forget forget forget you did
and now forever pay we know basic good and evil we will not sit
on your idealistic mediocrity falling through 70s and 80s to reach
colour we are the colour of the millennium we are supposed and
this generation – I will eat you and spit you out, no reverence for
history you all complain you created this attitude I didn't you
hippies, you peace-child, you smoker, you revolutionary where
are you now? Fighting Wal-Mart, whored social helpers you
babyboom, you sinners, you lust, you hurt, you watch, you laugh
Bill Clinton! I with you in Washington, where the media has
destroyed my life I with you in Washington, where women have
distracted me from my purpose I with you in Washington, giving
up my I for the group of I's I with you in Washington, for I am
human I with you in Washington, where we are blunted by the
same medial disease I with you in Washington, where I lie to
myself everyday I with you in Washington, where I generation
could turn me like yours did on you I with you in Washington, for
you are I president of I journey, I will not leave your legacy up to
measly men for you are the father of I sentiments and the martyr
of a hideous beauty millennium I shining in the colour I abandon
nothing for the sake of altruistic lack of vision I follow what I love
around the corner I lust I keep kicking it to the next level for Nate,
for love incarnate I smoker internal revolution of spirituality I
write and never never never forget I time in this youth I wander
and I wonder you find solitude oh son of I generation, little ones,
we can teach you most watch I, watch I very careful emotions run

moment to moment in youth we grow as you grew and ruin proper lives surrender to reality conform to love not for it human nature shit shit shit this deliberate manner in which we live, not taking advantage of moments for the future of our lives and family future stock options never open this is incorporation of past with unpredictability of future I is ok in that only if we can still live in the moment in minutes in seconds in I oh Moloch of country founded on the insecurity of other countries! Moloch of people lost for lack of self-evolution! Moloch of religion! Moloch of people who are unspiritual! Oh Moloch of you! Oh Moloch of who I could be! Oh Moloch I will never be! Where have you gone Joe DiMaggio? I tell you where you've gone

(thinking that you looked better before the makeover)

you are feeling elegantly wasted? I know I do • you are not supposed to • you are feeling so much better about your job this afternoon and are filled with a warm and satisfying glow • you are the head of a government that has just been voted back into power • you are constantly warning your ministers against arrogance • you are faced with the urgent issue of tackling the crisis in the public services – teaching, the health service and the police in particular • you are out there, walking around in the slowly emerging daylight • you are trying to get some sleep, it's the worst sound on earth • you are overcome with an insane urge to read through the entire weekly archives from start to finish • you are – > • you are not careful, it will turn your knees orange • you are thinking about buying this product, sign off and take a cold shower! This product is itchy, smelly and leaves streaks + spots! My boyfriend hated the taste and smell • you are self-conscious about them • you are a moron or not if you never talk to them? • "you are the best father for my children, how do I express that in one gift?" he smiled • you are very dangerous Miss Ross

(a bird no wait a plane no hell you're Superman)

you are ahead? What are Preparation A thru Preparation G? Do amphibians have to wait one hour before getting out of the water? If knees were backward, what would chairs look like? In a country of free speech, why are there phone bills? Why is it that when a man talks dirty to a woman, it's sexual harassment, but when a woman talks dirty to a man, it's $3? Why is it that when you are on the telephone, writing furiously and holding a finger up to tell the person who just came into your office to hold on a second, why do they ask "Do you have a minute"? Why is Greenland icy and Iceland green? If you take the wings off of a fly, does it become a walk? How come there aren't "B" batteries? If the post office has machines that can sort mail at a rate of thousands of times per minute, then why do they give it to a little old man on a bike to deliver? Why do doctors call what they do "practice"? Do you realize how many holes there could be if people would just take the time to take the dirt out of them? Have you ever imagined a world with no hypothetical situations? How can someone draw a blank? How can there be self-help "groups"? How come wrong numbers are never busy? How do they get a deer to cross at that yellow road sign? How do you know if honesty is the best policy unless you've tried some of the others? How do you throw away a garbage can? How does a Thermos know whether a drink should be hot or cold? How does the guy who drives the snow-plough get to work in the mornings? If a picture is worth a thousand words, what is a picture of a thousand words worth? If a word in the dictionary was misspelled, how would we know? If all the nations in the world are in debt, where did all the money go? If rabbits' feet are so lucky, then what happened to the rabbit? If you had a million Shakespeares in a room typing, would they write like a monkey? If you're in a vehicle going the speed of light, what happens when you turn on headlights? In court, why do they ask if you swear to tell the truth? If you're planning on lying, do they really think you'll tell them so? What do sheep count when they can't get to sleep? What does Geronimo say when he jumps out of a plane? If you are in Hell and you are mad at someone, where do you tell them to go? When cheese gets its picture taken, what does it say? When dog food is new and improved tasting, who tests it? What happened to the first six "Ups"? Why do kamikaze pilots wear helmets? How much would they pay the matador if the bull had no horns? How do "'do not walk on grass'" signs get there? Why do black olives come in cans and green olives come in jars? Before they invented drawing boards, what did they go back to? Do infants enjoy infancy as much as adults enjoy adultery? How do I set my laser printer on stun? How is it possible to have a civil war? If all the world is a stage, where is the audience sitting? If God dropped acid, would he see people? If love is blind, why is lingerie so popular? If the #2 pencil is the most popular, why is it still #2? If you ate pasta and antipasta, would you still be hungry? Why are haemorrhoids called "haemorrhoids" instead of "asteroids"? Why is the alphabet in that order? Is it because of that song? Why is there an expiration date on sour cream? If most car accidents occur within five miles of home, why doesn't everyone just move 10 miles away? If man evolved from monkeys and apes, why do we still have monkeys and apes? What happens to an 18-hour bra after 18 hours? Where are the germs that cause "good" breath? Why aren't there ever any guilty bystanders? Why can't you make another word using all the letters in "anagram"? Why didn't Noah swat those two mosquitoes? Why do "fat chance" and "slim chance" mean the same thing? Why do hot dogs come ten to a package and hot dog buns only eight? Why do mattresses have springs, if they aren't made for jumping on? Why do they call it life insurance? Why do tourists go to the top of tall buildings and then put money in telescopes so they can see things on the ground in close-up? Why do we kill people for killing people to show that killing is wrong? Why is it considered necessary to nail down the lid of a coffin? Why is it that night falls but day breaks? Why is it you must wait until night to call it a day? Why is your index finger the same size as your nostrils? How do you remove a club soda stain? What if the Hokey Pokey is what it's all about? Why do you need a driver's license to buy liquor when you can't drink and drive? When your pet bird sees you reading the newspaper, does he wonder why you are just sitting there, staring at carpeting? Why is there only one monopolies and mergers commission? If you get wrapping paper for a present, how do you know when to stop unwrapping? Why do they report power outages on TV? If 7-Eleven is open 24-7 and 365 days a year why do they have locks on their doors? If you mix Milk of Magnesia with vodka and orange juice, do you get a Phillips screwdriver? Why isn't there mouse-flavoured cat food? How can something be "new" *and* "improved"? Whose cruel idea was it to put the "s" in lisp?

(an uninterrupted series of dots that hasn't come to terms with being a line yet)

you are only a spectator reflecting on it from the outside, reflecting that outside, produced by it, reproducing it • you are the one who can learn • you are smarter than me • you are the most sleepiest man strong song composite wind is in the corn cornering, a man in a fever is no trifling thing if you sit in the Jim Crow • you are in it • you are never likely to meet • you are unlikely to get an answer • you are turned on by Larter's toothy smiles • you are finished; maybe you don't even have a name yet • you are going to play *Vampire: The Masquerade* • you are the first to break this!! I have asked RobinD not to discuss with anyone else how it was broken • you are belittling me or my efforts to the community, think again • you are describing a contest • you are belittling me or my efforts to the community, think again I don't believe I have addressed anyone by name so far • you are saying I have • you are certainly free to disagree with my position on this matter • you are saying the subject matter is serious, but the format of the question is not? I'm more than a little curious how that works • you are entitled to gratefulness *and* anger, but thank God he was able to walk away from it • you are although my two older boys put us through some tests at times – my youngest hasn't got there yet he's nine but I'm sure his day is coming • you are thankful he is okay, but angry that he did something so stupid in the first place • you are entitled to both feelings • you are familiar with the game show *Jeopardy*, the category can be coronary disease • you are approaching all this from a completely different angle than we are and perhaps that is where the disagreement came to being • you are 20 seconds away from having access!

(an ill-used neural cluster removed to get at a deep-seated brain tumour)*

you are 50 feet up in the air and trying to walk on a rope no more than an inch across! • you are expected to handle whatever comes your way, ready or not • you are fortunate enough to have these kinds of individuals in your life, don't be shy about calling on them for help and support • you are having trouble viewing this message, please let us know • you are relying on recent information, as you should be • you are a brave and special person and I will miss your journal very much • you are an inspirational and courageous man • you are a hero to me! All the very best to you – you are in my thoughts and prayers • you are an inspiration to us all • you are an amazing man • you are in this family's prayers every day • you are going through something, I feel that your words have helped me understand more and hopefully become a better, more caring, understanding worker • you are an inspiration • you are such a fighter and give inspiration and strength to so many • you are not defeated but won a great victory – your light will shine on • you are an inspiration to us all – I have been deeply humbled by your constant bravery and optimism • you are a very brave and selfless person, and if I were in your situation, I hope I would be capable of being even half as brave as you • you are in our thoughts • you are a strong and inspirational person and I send my love to you and wish you the best for the future • you are in my heart and thoughts • you are brilliant • you are unaware of the ripple effect • you are truly a remarkable person • you are that rarest of individuals, someone who has really made a difference in this world • you are truly a great inspiration, and the most courageous person • you are courageous and strong and I am sure that your children will grow to be very proud of you • you are you • you are really a wonderful person • you are superb for all time

(fading away when you would rather be burning out)

you are still there • you are there, hello, whoever you are • you are
ready to be helped through this, I'll be right here• you are dry and
cool • "you are out of touch," replies the mad alchemist; "Didn't
you see the landlord in the main hall today? Ever since he raised
the price of blackcurrant and lemonade, he's been one of us" • you
are a lesbian ferret-owning amputee who likes line-dancing • you
are fading, there's more of a chance for someone to catch you, love
you, be with you, on the path to your demise • you are all passed
out

(a linguistic trap set to catch some good eatin' possum)*

you are a redneck if: • you are at work • you and your wife are both in the same grade • you are still holding on to Confederate money because you think the south will rise again • you are bombarded with ads for penis enlargement, hit with spyware, and receive messages from some person in Africa claiming to be a prince who wants to share his fortune with you • you are followed by federal agents of the Bureau Of Alcohol Tobacco And Firearms, and the only thing you worry about is if you can lose them or not • you are waking up with both a black eye and a hickey • you are steadily wrecking this blog for all the poor people who are trying to write something and the rest of the visitors who want to read something interesting • you are having marital problems because your wife never lets you win at arm wrestling • you are good at metal working, you might be a machinist • you are famous for your homemade squash wine • you are having a yard sale • you are allowed to bring your dog to work • you are still upset about *Gunsmoke* being cancelled • you are not allowed to mention the game warden's name in the house • you are not hauling anything • you are considered an expert on worm beds • you are turned on by a woman who can field dress a deer • you are looking for sex, dirty language and mindless violence – sorry, you won't find it here

(eleven benevolent elephants)

you are telling a story • you are my only hope • you are interested in fifteen years or so • you are fired • you are a mo-ron! A potential H-bomb! • you are an oracle but you've got to go to consultants for all the tough questions • you are in luck, oh unfortunate mortal, for the qualifications for the presidency and for the managership of a Dairy Queen Brazier are remarkably similar • you are in too big of a hurry to go the normal route • you are not careful, you may get caught; however, this may actually help • you are one of those Pythonites too, aren't you? • "you are in love – that fat woman Warrington?" he enquired • you are reading so fast • you are the dancer, within you the answer if only you'll dare • you are right, Kris was surely a prick at times, but I think what we see with Kris is the gradual (and painfully slow!) development of a shallow person into something more noble • you are exempt from attending, think again • "you are a goner anyway!" The man thinks about this for a minute and decides that the genie's right • you are gonna love this – "Yellow River"! A woman from the University of Hamburg, Germany, sent this one: Why does it take four premenstrual women to change a light bulb? "Cause it does, right?" Cheryl Lynne Bradley, President, Tarot Canada • you are psychic, think "Honk"! from 22-year-old Alfiya in Central Asia, who read this in a magazine: after 10 days of delay even menstruation is a holiday • you are the wind beneath my wings • you are on this site anyway • you are two hours late I don't watch movies with lots of gore don't need instant replay to remember the score don't go "yeeuuukkkk"! scroll down for more vampire jokes • you are lying, you look at the ceiling • you are crazy, so why don't you just open up that discussion • you are a very talented person who is ready to come back to work • you are playing on a soap, you are probably only going to be doing the role for six weeks, six months, but you are never going to make it to the six year mark • you are difficult • you are hard to work with • you are leaving, be in the middle of a marriage that is disintegrating and look like the cheeriest camper of the summer • you are going to be very good in this part • you are doing tape, it is so hard for one person to do two parts • you are talking to Dorian, aren't you? Okay, Dorian • you are so funny, such wit • you are working with all new actors • "you are my fifth Cassie!" • you are going to do 51 pages in one show – the script is only 100 pages – there is no better person to do it with • you are not imitating these people but you look and watch their essence • you are rehearsing is being promoted as "fun for the whole dysfunctional family!" • you are hearing "Roger Howarth, call extension 352" • you are in a holding pattern • you are on your back in bed for 10 days or you are in the hospital • you are just not a good soldier • you are not going to say "No" • you are moving to the plastic surgery capital of the world, would you consider having your face done? Strasser – I couldn't make my living if my face didn't wiggle

(damp semen soaked into the centrefold)

"you are really getting into this, ain't you, Mulder? You like it? You like to suck cock?" asked Spender as Mulder returned to deep-throating his cock • "you are into all that back-to-nature crap, Agent Mulder?" Kersh sneered • you are one of my best people • you are my one and only, I promise • you are such a slut! Marita, it's time to get to work • you are in place • you are good, Fox, I won't put on a head mask, blindfold, or gag • you are going to lick Marita's pussy • you are going to feel me • you are safe now • "you are awake!" Mulder turned his head to see who it was • you are wearing a gag! I'm glad Alex called me to come down and help you out • "you are out of your mind!" "I am not on drugs! Listen to me!" he was glaring angrily at his mother • you are telling them about your own love "B-b-b-but mom, I…" Mulder couldn't finish his sentence • you are going to wear heels like that you should learn to walk in them • you are going to have anal intercourse, at least do it properly • you are going to get, so just keep counting • you are awake, Mulder • you are wearing a latex face mask, it's part of the package that you'll never grok – he manages to stifle an on-edge giggle • you are such a bad liar! Let's just say that Skinner and I have some common acquaintances • you are good, we'll all enjoy a nice romp when we get to your master's cabin • you are obedient, I won't put them back on • "you are going to really feel some pain," hissed the deeper-voiced person • you are the one in charge • you are not able to control your penis and ass – apparently anyone can come by and have their way with you • you are bad at it, the old lady insisted, seizing the initiative • you are curious • you are wondering why you, what makes you special, how come you are involved and I can't answer any of that • you are going to do what? Mickey thought • you are a demon, a high-ranking fiend, he wanted to say but couldn't • you are consistent • you are vacillating

(a registered trademark)*

you are like most people, you simply concluded that since you thought of it, other people had probably thought of it as well • you are in it for the long haul • you are going to use it as a legal weapon, surely you'd like it to be as sharp as possible? • you are speaking to what it is you want to make more specifically • you are making the disclosure • you are interested – use what knowledge you've got and do some digging around without disclosing to others what you are actually looking for • you are serious about this and have been prepared to put your own time and money behind it • you are that the product will sell • you are looking to cash in via the government • you are in compliance • you are looking to cut down on your intake of headache medication • you are trying to cut to the chase? • you are probably eligible for very few • you are not a kid anymore (supreme arbiter and lawgiver of music)†

you are looking at further endless interpretive dilemmas, not
clear answers • you are assigning an ongoing task of interpretation
to the other pillars • you are so clever! • you are so right • you are
doing them no service by merely pointing to the fact that
constructionism fails to protect them with exacting perfection
while failing to bother with analysis on the obvious problem that
rival systems fail even further • you are trying to have a discussion
which fails to agree at the most fundamental level here, whether
people can disagree with each other without one person being
inherently dishonest or not, one cannot get to any reasonable
common ground in the later arguments without first resolving
the initial sting see Dworkin's laws of empire • you are on the left
or the right, maybe • you are claiming to be completely correct
about the countries that have used a juvenile death penalty
despite the fact that your list of countries has changed • you are
detecting although I'm at a loss to see how anything I wrote
suggests any sort • you are making a critical error here which is
that texts somehow have meaning outside of context • you are
trying to determine what, from a gods'-eye-view, is the reasonable
answer to our problem *now* – that's the *only* way appeal to
intent drops out • you are reasonable to understand what you are
up to • you are not saying that • you are quite right that it wouldn't
be the no-holds-barred disagreement we might have if we were
freely deciding here and now what we thought • you are a fool,
you suck, conceivably • you are not really being unfair to so-called
originalism, but if we abandon it, I'm a moving target and will call
what I want something else • you are back with the priesthood •
you are stupid • you are asking him not to do his job in the first
place • you are bound by the text's "original meaning" if you can
figure it out: maybe original understanding is a reminder that
words can change their meaning over time, so we should be
historically disciplined by facts about contemporary usage • you
are really concerned with enlightening yourself to the answer, you

really owe it to yourself to examine the piece • you are suggesting either or both of those things: • you are holding: I wouldn't want you tearing my web • you are waiting, you don't expend much energy • you are saying you disagree with this guy and think flag burning should be illegal? Me: Illegal? I never said that • you are making money off killing people with deadly drugs and you know it's deadly but you don't say anything, shouldn't you be able to be sued for it? • you are interested in the story you can easily • you are probably thinking "Is this what Thomas Jefferson really would have said?" Obviously no one knows what his exact words would be, but I've based much of the material in all of the Thomas Jefferson LiveJournal updates on a lengthy study of the thousands of letters Jefferson has written, even down to a point of attempting to preserve Jefferson's diction • you are breaking the law, no matter if the police give you a certain amount of grace • you are quoting Sammy Hagar? I'm not sure I've spelled his name right • you are not abstaining from all appearance of evil? Then the question is how slow do have to go before you are abstaining from the appearance of evil? Then beyond that, especially in Philadelphia and Washington DC where I live and travel, in your slowing down will you cause accidents and death? When you have 6 lanes of bumper-to-bumper traffic going north on I-95 running at 70+ mph and someone decides to slow down to the speed limit of 55; accidents happen • you are conflating forensic innocence and actual innocence • you are confused or lost then say you are confused or lost, so that I may simplify things for you • you are faced with a dilemma that involves the nature of God Himself • you are not fulfilling your purpose for existence by being on this blog • you are right that appealing to tradition of any kind is not an argument • you are searching for a political philosophy that's completely sound from a logical standpoint • you are aware, that's impossible • you are in very safe hands • you are retarded • you are sitting too close to your screen • you are forced to make arguments that

233

freaking stupid to defend your policy, your policy is a really bad idea • you are willing to do with their education using the theory of evolution, you should first acquaint yourself with the principle of deceleration • you are justified in doing so • you are living in a fantasy world • you are feeling depressed, take two shots of tequila and call me in the morning • you are determined to make the answer yes • you are paying for the privilege of being lied to, conned, brainwashed and deceived; kept occupied with masses of trivia that conceals much subversive material

(woman, hear you roar)

you are all wet! • you are in for war! Who do you think keeps us
going through the days? Do you think I'm out there, soakin' up
rays??? From career woman to housewife, I've got it down pat! I'm
darned near perfect • you are one of these people, then you will
be pissed off by this • you are so proud to be women, yet you are
not women • you are eating the womb of a tree • you are doing
Private Ryan a favour 'cause you are trying to stop the war • you
are making a difference • you are not making a difference and just
pissing people off so shut the fuck up, go home and play some
video games • you are a real pro-life feminist – quick 10-step
checklist • you are a pro-life feminist too! • you are articulate,
versatile and adroit • you are encouraged to cultivate your natural
communication skills • you are accommodating and obliging •
you are very good at perceiving, comparing and communicating
• you are much more objective than most people and probably
more liberal in your thinking • you are here: • you are young, if
you had to go to church, there's always some old guy standing
behind you sort of mouthing the words? Everyone else is singing
tunefully and behind you [it's] "on-ward-Chris-tian-sol-diers-
mar-ching" • you are in a room with five people, four of whom
are talking rationally – like "OK, come on! Push!" – and there's one
person screaming at the top of their lungs, which are you going
to pay attention to? Men loving aliens loving men – two music
videos making the rounds now offer oddly contrary vistas into
alien realms • you are paying for them, but how accountable are
they for your dollar? • you are on your own and you find that you
are always the one to organize events, run errands for relatives
and otherwise find ways to put your needs last, ask for assistance

(never going to amount to a hill of beans in the world)

you are a fine looking man! Where do you live! Write back! Don't you love the Internet? I like it very much because it lets me meet people all over the world! Like you! Bye, Tracy and Mahir wrote back!!! Hi* Thanks for your e-mail and picture* I live Turkey Izmir – Izmir nice town – 4 million near the sea I invite you my home – my home – your home I belive we could be good friend* where are you live* write me about you* I wait you I kiss you – kissessssssssssss and hugssssssssss Mahir's response was so formulaic, suspicions were raised that he might be an auto-responder and of course "Mahir Cagri" translates from the Turkish into "skilful invitation" • you are not the man I had fallen in love with!!! You never e-mail me anymore • you are too busy e-mailing all your other Internet girlfriends • you are lucky the bar is open • you are disgustingly lazy • you are in the audience • you are going to see of him until he emerges on the other side of his Atlantic with his verb in his mouth • you are turning into a penguin! Stop it!" • you are getting on that plane • you are getting on that plane with Victor where you belong • you are not with him, you'll regret it • "you are on?" "I have no conviction, if that's what you mean" • you are the only one in Casablanca who has even less scruples than I • you are not with him, you'll regret it • you are spewing, ill-informed, inaccurate, downright stupid comments from people who don't know FA about what they're discussing • you are an exception • you are saying that we should just take what we get and like it rather than expect or demand that journalists adhere to their supposed "sacred" trust and we shouldn't criticize incompetence • you are welcome to it • you are involved either as the patient, a close family member or a review board doctor • you are in for even worse times ahead over there in the US

(bad advice foisted on some lovesick puppy)

you are sitting outside at one of Houston's fine cafés or bistros, it is not uncommon for a grackle to land on the chair next to you and stare at you with its calculating yellow eyes • you are both correct • you are really not going to like what happens next • you are dead • you are such an a**hole I don't want to talk about it – go away, I'm still building up steam – well it's been almost 20 years since consumer's' reports reviewed girlfriends, circa August 1972 • you are able to spend • you are good-looking, have a commanding personality and a good sense of humour, you will have the resources to obtain a fancy, high-end model • you are ugly, smell bad and wear polyester clothes, your choices are more limited • you are able to spend • you are good-looking, have a healthy rack and long hair, you will have the resources to obtain a fancy, high-end model • you are ugly, smell bad and resemble a boy, even with the brain of a genius your choices are more limited • you are not in the habit of wearing any when we go out in the evening • you are a young teenager with a repressed sex drive • you are safe from the law! * in hotels in Sioux Falls, South Dakota, every room is required to have twin beds • you are a single, divorced or widowed woman, you can't parachute on Sunday afternoons • you are obviously wrong • "you are a bit young for that?" He slaps another hundred on the counter and says "I want one of your women" • you are sorry you had me neutered

(an axiom proved false)

you are giving more credence/weight to Kevin • you are fond of saying – in fact, the opposite is true! What few psychological studies have been performed on those who claim "abduction" experiences shows them to be no more or less neurotic than anyone else in the population • you are being very objective • you are either inconsistent or incomplete • you are invited to imagine yourself doing something that you just couldn't do • you are willing to say that that person no longer has cognitive states? If someone is blind and can no longer see the world; if they're invalided and are no longer able to have interactions with the world; if they have severe cerebral palsy and no longer have connections through their body with the outside world; if they have mental illnesses, loss of affect • you are not, in fact, the one reading this entry • you are taking part in an experiment being run by hyper-intelligent white mice • you are allowed to either take just box B or to take both box A and box B • you are just another human, so if you take both boxes you get £1000; if you take just box B, then you get £1,000,000 • you are given the following question: • you are a complete moron • you are an Objectivist! With what non-sense do you propose to counter the evidence of the senses? • you are relying on may later turn out to be inconsistent, so it's good to keep a record • you are absolutely confident that (1) it is correct and (2) the reader will automatically agree that it is correct • you are sorry – it provides a means for guaranteeing your claims once and for all

(the cruellest month)

you are still in for a mind-blowing experience reading this book
• you are not suffering from any particularly debilitating stressful
event, this information may seem obvious • you are checking out
this section • you are as full of pep and vigour as you would like
to be! • you are bound to have fun! If you haven't started writing
a diary as yet, get your act together and start your very own
personal journal today! Write about anything you want, after all
it's your own thoughts

(an error in grammar identified by the latest in word-processing technology)

you are the best teacher I never met in past three years so I like your class and I would like to show as more about conputer and English pratice • you are a "coot" idiot if you don't know a "messy" good tune when you hear it • you are not "one of the guys" and it's often difficult to understand what is being said • you are all set; "central reservation," highway median; "dual carriageway," a divided highway; and "coach," a bus for travelling long distances • "you are a dog"? It's going to get easier • you are not connected, you are not connected • you are not connected, get connected

(flown to your destination on Delta Air Lines)

you are a little flexible on your itinerary and you stand a good chance of getting what you want • you are that unhappy • you are in frames and wish to replicate the target • you are not sure where you want to go • you are travelling with two small children, decide now which one you love more

(the book in the spirit machine)

you are selling your soul when you accept employment in the corporate media and when you are then rewarded with status, privilege and even power • you are in the centre, that knows when you are on the beam or off the beam • you are dating, too! But fear not! You too can learn to roll with the punches, even on a date with a totally rockin' chick or guy – if you are a girl or a gay guy • you are at an all-you-can-eat BBQ or a similar location where being messy is the point, you won't mind some sauce on your nose • you are on a regular date, trying to maintain some sense of decorum and not look like you just rolled out of kindergarten with the other little piggies • you are gazing into each other's eyes, or you are both sitting there shyly trying to figure out if ordering dessert is a good idea or you should just suggest walking over to the movie, even the most careful and steady hands can slip up • you are drunk • you are a music lover and may want to investigate my CD collection • you are who you say you are • you are a very entertaining writer! • you are not able to accomplish both with suave, debonair charm and true emotional feeling within his words • you are a collection of networks, constantly feeding information back and forth across the line to the millions of networks that make up your "world" • you are destined to the resurrection, why not enjoy it!?! • you are merely "present" on this earth; God's offer of hope of a free, indestructible life is yours without cost and more secure than anything mankind can imagine or compare to any earthly condition • you are unable to be interested on your own • you are saved or lost by others' deeds • you are waiting for the Holy Spirit to push you forward might I suggest that day will never come

(a Dadaist who needs to love and be loved)

you are a worried girl and you wrote to us because we turn you
on and you want our bodies and/or you think we are cute, here is
your own personal section of the letter: the answer to any and all
questions is, yes, we love you even if you are fat, with pimples •
you are very hep and swinging and you wrote to us on a piece of
toilet paper, this section is for you: keep up the good work • you
are different • you are interested in this worthwhile program of,
let's call it "self-help," please be advised that our work can be
continued only if your membership is kept paid yearly and we
have periodic reports of your activities within the context of our
program • you are glad that they can think? Ever say you loved
'em? Ever let 'em watch you drink? Ever wonder why your daughter
looked so sad? It's such a drag to have to love a plastic mom and
dad, "plastic people" therefore revisited, adding moisture cream
and facial lotion to the goo and whatnot • you are not apathetic
to or swayed from who you truly are • you are what you is, blend
together in flower punk's head to form a hallucinogenic mish-
mash behind one low, up-front character fantasizing about
love-child utopia and royalty cheques • "you are fat!" might seem
non-sarcastic; but he doesn't believe it for a second • you are a
guest at Camp Reagan • you are the slayer! • you are cold • you are
just jealous • you are two people • you are ready for the big leagues,
let me know • you are trying to Scully me! • you are the mystery
guy, you tell me • you are looking a little worn around the eyes •
you are doing is wrong • you are brave and resourceful in a crisis
episode • you are gonna use wisdom • you are grounded! • you are
not to leave your room at any time! Clear? • you are expelled • you
are fired Giles Episode 47 • you are covered in slime • you are
going to have a nice, fun, normal evening! • you are spoiled, Buffy
• you are not alone anymore • you are the patriarch • you are done
• you are so strong and proud of it thanks to Mr. Apollo, follow
Mr. Apollo, everybody knows he's the greatest benefactor of
mankind, follow Mr. Apollo, everybody knows that a healthy

body makes a healthy mind 'cos he's the strongest man the world has ever seen and if you take his courses, he'll make you big and rough and you can kick the sand right back in their faces • you are all going to be crucified • you are so right • "you are not going to like it!" "What's the answer?" I asked • you are trying to know what really happened historically • you are going to get drunk again? Louis Jordan's song returned like a headache, a mild eructation at the back of the throat: memory of something told from experience, something not mediated via all this second-guessing of everyone else's point of view • you are an ignoramus • you are going mad, semen, diabolical rasp: "They're what you fuck you mean" • you are qualified to engage me in a conversation about Karl Marx's concept of monetary exchange and its relation to humanism? I was going to ask you the same question • you are moulded by the very same ideological formation! No way was he the simple proletarian promised by his apparel, thought Froth • you are taken through the genie's ethereal world • you are in Chicago • you are into the domination fantasies • you are interested in the band, you should get *Leben Im Niemandsland*, which is kind of like a best-of album • you are likely to miss the happy nuptials altogether • you are risking something by doing this • you are willing to take those chances • you are trimming their hair or shaving them, or what have you • you are talking about at all and would you ever entertain the idea of maybe making it a song that might invite more people into the world of it? Vis-a-vis, why don't you fuckin' get some words together that someone else could identify with if they're sitting over in Cleveland? • you are hoping to build, I think the song will eventually speak to you in ways that maybe aren't readily apparent when you are starting to work with it • you are working on a short story and thinking do you need the main protagonist to say this there, or should they kind of shut up and work the angle of mystery into the story a little more?

(pre-conceived by Boethius and William the Conqueror but have no clue as to what Surrealism is really on about)*

you are probably right when you say that economic freedom enables freedom to experiment with form • you are writing stuff that's as good as anyone's, as good as much of that which is getting published in major outlets • you are getting down • you are good at it • you are a celebrity and I can't help admiring you • you are as strange in person as you are on TV • you are cast back down into the depths • you are fighting Napster now too, huh? • you are so fucking dead to me • you are ever in the market for a wizard hat, might I recommend talking to this lady? • you are willing to go along for the ride • you are going to spend so much time cataloguing his decline • you are underwhelmed • you are not going to get my favourite books or ones that I would necessarily recommend to others • you are probably going to chuckle, but Alan Watts's book on the taboo against knowing who you are was seriously formative • you are going with this • you are willing to go along for the ride • you are not dying the way Chloe is dying • you are underwhelmed if that's a word

(hoping that you will never have to hear that fucker read his damn poem again)

you are shit • you are shit • you are shit outta luck!! B1: submit s1 you are an ass with no class! B1: submit s1 what!!!!! B1: submit s1 I promised you a poem so I went through my book I couldn't find anything so I took another look this time I looked within my heart that is where I found the words to start I promised you a poem but where do I begin there are so many things I need to fill in we had lost touch for such a long time so many things have happened in this life of mine but through all that's gone on and all the days passed by I've never forgotten you and even though we've grown apart you will always have a special place in my heart I promised you a poem not knowing where to begin now I write you this poem not knowing where to end B1: submit s1 when I go down the stairs I expect to die when I go up the stairs I expect to live either way I have a railing B1: submit s1 here should be a picture of my favourite apple • you are too • you are done, you can delete it • you are the American dream as long as everything that is you pads the pocket of the right people • you are interested making sure to remove the word delete • you are in suspension • you are not worried about legalities of that kind of thing for new poems • you are all so simple • you are here criticizing them because you don't think what they are saying is a good thing • you are helpless – futilely trudging on, writing • you are exposed, she has you beaten, whipped "Babe … I have to go to work," you say, already too far along • you are so kind • you are her boyfriend • you are at work • you are insane you jump up and down crazy crazy you try to barrel through the fucking security guard like a wall the fucking thug don't you see that fucking thug he is going to fucking rape my girl don't you see that fucking monster you pound at him with your shoulder ahhhh you don't have enough strength rage and fire ahhhh and blood is coming out of your skin ahhhh your teeth snapping your girl is wiggling fast ahhhh and then you can't see anything ahhhh and the guard throws you into the parking lot • you are wondering what has brought this new burst of energy, enlightenment and determination: Wilson Phillips • you are a winner • you are anything but the best • you are in a room full of people so you know it'd be tactless • you are not familiar with this unique practice, it involves a mass amount of beer, a few canoes, a sunburn and four or five hours on the water • you are Jerome, bitch, don't forget that • "you are in a really bad porno?" Goose: "No, it's really good" (in more closets than you wish to admit)†

you are not going to be fair • you are a closet Kenny G fan or an
outspoken diehard, *The Ultimate Kenny G* is the most complete
definitive up-to-date collection by this brilliant saxophonist • you
are a true music lover by that I mean you just love music, not noise
as is given out by rock songs that provide just temporary thrill
than fizz out • you are smooth, you need to communicate • you
are trying to get him in bed • you are easily shocked • you are so
witty – humour like that needs to be shared • you are a geek, eh?
The first step is to admit to yourself your geekiness • you are a geek
• you are a geek • you are a geek, so use the universal geek code!
Using this special code will allow you to let other un-closeted
geeks know who you are in a simple, codified statement • you are
able to construct your own overall geek code • you are living an
unconventional life • you are right it does seem like "it" until you
sometimes smarten up • you are lucky enough to hold one of six
billion shovels • you are running low on air pollutants • you are
dismayed to discover one angry letter from a superior and six
hundred forwarded messages from your drinking buddies • you
are ready to get to work • you are just kidding – you actually have
two gay friends • you are insignificant • you are a male trapped in
a 1950s mentality • you are anything that you want to be – a
billionaire firing young go-getters, single and faced with a choice
between 50 chiselled faces, trapped on a desert island among half
dressed big-breasted women, a news anchor, a forensics cop or
later in the evening, a porn star

(someone with the debilitating habit of cutting against the grain)

you are hereby forewarned • you are getting a sufficient amount •
you are right, but it does sound time consuming • you are crazy
to smoke, can smoking make you crazy? • you are over the age of
30, there's something you ought to know about your muscles:
they're probably shrinking • you are seen as not doing enough •
you are of the mind that a wellness clinic is all about gossamer,
candles and chanting, you may be in for a rude awakening • you
are properly understood • you are not careful, as intellectual pride
can very easily become mistaken for emotional honour • you are
back where you began and wondering how you got there • you
are afraid you might be wrong • you are more cooperative and not
so likely to fight over territory if you know there is plenty to go
around • you are not only likely to have a taste for the unusual in
terms of emotional or sexual satisfaction, you are also likely to
have difficulty getting enough of it or exactly the right kind • you
are asking for trouble and you won't get to first base in the way of
solving the problem that this raises • you are allowed to go as far
out as you want to satisfy one or both of you, everything will be
OK • you are still not satisfied • you are chasing the concept instead
of living the experience • you are dealing with such affairs • you
are intolerant of mistakes in the outside world and you will have
the balance just right • you are ready to fire it • you are on the right
course, or at least on the one you believe you are on • you are not
careful in the way you use it • you are stagnating and it will mean
that others can look to the two of you for inspiration and new
ideas • you are never going to get there • you are ready to harness
it – like a wild horse – you can ride it far • you are the founding
ancestors of an age undreamed of in human history • you are on
drugs? We have three free programs for you here in this county! •
you are fired

(going going gone)

you are not up for eating your little barnyard friends, so how about just relaxing in the sun and catching some rays • you are at the beach, go ahead and learn about crustaceans • you are into it, deep • you are interested in participating more with this organization • you are also buying a large handgun, this is true • you are in big trouble, according to certain humourless readers • you are not convinced; read the next one

(a likely consumer of rubber nipples)

you are able to successfully disconnect your brain while watching action movies • you are a nitpicker whose favourite movies were all made before 1950 • you are getting this newsletter in error and for some perplexing reason wish to leave us • you are going to hate several children • you are home, stimpy • you are away from home • you are home away from home • you are working in the kitchen • you are not convinced of the dangers and leave the wheels on and you should really be sure to keep the door to any stairway locked • you are prepared when flooding occurs • you are sure all parts are working smoothly • you are in doubt … drain the case, flush it with solvent and refill with clean oil • you can spread talcum powder on the handle to prevent your hands from getting all horny • you notice a shortness of breath, unusual swelling of the sting area, or feel nauseous • you are bitten by a rat and it's time to wash the wound with soap and water and see a doctor immediately • you are sure all parts are working smoothly • you are in doubt • you are sure all parts are working smoothly • you are in doubt • you are sure all parts are working smoothly • you are in doubt • you are sure all parts are working smoothly • you are in doubt• you are sure all parts are working smoothly • you are in doubt• you are sure all parts are working smoothly • you are in doubt • you are high and alone and your mission in life is just to clean little unimportant things like the TV screen • you are stoned enough, but you never seem to get where you are going • you are watching, looking out at all this simultaneous movement, taking in the panorama of the ever-changing street • you are stoned, but decide what you want to do before you smoke • you are pumping forward and feeling your muscles enlarging and pushing you on, with the sweat pouring out of you • you are moving more slowly • you are moving when you are high, it's the greatest experience • you are stoned: the wind against your face, the muscles that you use becoming visible in isolation • you are gliding along in that canoe • you are high; everything's great, you are relaxed and you want to embrace the whole world, you are so happy • you are stoned and realize that I can be incredibly depressing • you are having the munchies and thinking that you will be eating away from home and you forgot to pack some wet towelettes or wipes for cleaning surfaces and hands • you are not sure a particular food is cold enough, so take its temperature with a food thermometer • you are certain that your water supply is safe • you know that substitutions are easy • you are making scrambled eggs or using a beaten egg to coat cutlets – use whatever size egg you have on hand • you are baking a cake, or making a custard – you will want to measure the volume of your substitute eggs and use the equivalent amount to what the large eggs would yield: 1 large egg, beaten = 3¼ tablespoons; 2 large eggs, beaten = 6½ tablespoons ¼ cup plus 2½ tablespoons; 3 large eggs, beaten — 9⅔ tablespoons ½ cup plus 1½ tablespoons; 4 large eggs, beaten = 12¾ tablespoons ¾ cup plus 1 teaspoon; 5 large eggs, beaten = 1 cup • you are luckily still stoned • you are lucky enough to get 10,000 years on a bakery planet • you are at it hard; let's see some polish on those shoes, mister • you are aware the ghost of Elvis has been haunting cows • you are going to shatter the illusion like that and I'm not going to take you seriously anymore • you are offended by this or you are under the legal age of consent in your country; do not read on

(a long-lost jazz score that no one would have played anyway)*

you are in the shower, grab the morning java • you are the soft generation – the first generation to not have to truly worry about warfare on our soil, and so you started the "America is the greatest evil on earth" belief because you have no true sense of what evil, or poverty, or totalitarianism really are • you are correct, I should have pointed that out • you are conflating lots of stuff here • you are totally in control • you are coloured green, trapped inside • you are locked up airtight but your self-control is leaking • you are seeking • you are somewhere in between what you want and what you seem • you are a shadow in her hands • you are beautiful in my eyes • you are familiar with "Never Talk To Strangers" off that album, meet its first cousin here, "Picking Up After You" • you are looking for more of the woozy jazz you heard on *Alice*, here's a good place to find it • "You Are What You Is" has a revised and inferior version called "Drafted Again" • you are a big Zappa fan and have never heard it, hear it now • you are best off resisting it

(a last will and testament)

you are still alive as of 1/09, so please rewrite your will at your earliest opportunity • you are a great guy and I hope to see you in the forum later • you are doing a great moderating job of every forum you participate in and I've many good comments about you • you are never wrong • you are really helpful also • you are damn good • you are not there • you are unconscious and unable to communicate with your family • you are aware that this would be an ideal time to discuss artificial life support, or unnecessary prolonged life support, with your lawyer • you are just a person • you are hot shit • you are a nincompoop • you are a whole person – you don't want to get stuck in one part of you • you are God or something • you are an asshole • you are standing somewhere but that does not necessarily mean you are standing in a line • you are prepared to suck their cock, or cocks, as the case may be • you are violating their property rights • you are going to blow it away • you are an attractive person but that does not necessarily mean you are someone's babe, or honey, or sweetie • you are taking a walk in the neighbourhood but that does not necessarily mean you are taking a vacation • you are prepared to be a captive audience … or victim

(an unceremonious exit)*

you are always thinking "I wish I would have done this, I wish I would have run a little faster, a little farther" • you are young but it doesn't matter • you are lurking, they know • you are most likely to inadvertently injure someone, or have someone tear a chunk out of you • you are on a Mac and your keyboard is set to "Canadian" change the settings in the control panel so the keyboard is set to "US" standards • you are now amongst the initiated • you are now the only person hanging out in an empty room • you are picking your nose • you are not solely responsible for some piece of bad news, you are more at risk of taking the fall • you are backed into a corner, you have to figure out how to get to that number, Lewis says • you are not a failure until you start blaming someone else, when will we realize this? In fact it's not the fault of Indians, it's quite frankly instilled in them from their childhood, since they are babies!! • you are a loser in life so blame your parents • you are lucky to witness an accident on the Indian's roads, you will see that both of the two involved in the accident will accept their mistake • you are plain confused, when you are feeling lonely or simply, when u want to be with someone you know loves you as much as you do • you are least expecting it, your friends shatter your life with a few, only a few chosen words – you stand there looking at your life crumbling to pieces like it's happening to someone else • you are down, everyone around you should abandon you and term you as a failure and not let you have another chance?? This is injustice and if the "wise" selectors think that they will get away with this at all, then they don't know Indians that well • you are on week 165 • you are innocent, he said, handing it over • you are as clever as I am, it's not hard to trick goody-two-shoes • you are under age 18, always check with your parents before you submit anything to us! This page contains paid advertisements; characters, logos, names and all related indicia are trademarks • you are contorting the facts to fit the story

255

appendix (a few from deeper in)

(all hat and no cattle)

you are a card-carrying member of the John Birch Society, the ARA and the "kill a freak for Jesus" chapter in your town • you are sure that Judge Bork got a raw deal • you are 40 years old and have never dated, let alone been married, because you're saving yourself for Margaret Thatcher • you are in the "top 1 percent" income bracket • you are going to be someday, somehow • you are too drunk to fish and too dumb to hunt • you are in favour of cutting taxes on investments, even though the only investments you ever made were in lottery tickets because someday one of them suckers will pay off and then you'll be rich too! Yee-haw! • you are sure that one day you are going to hit the jackpot and be one of them • you are glad to see things back to normal • you are still mad because "Rummy" Rumsfeld and Dubya won't let you play with their guns • you are on Medicare, need prescription drug help and still voted for the village idiot • you are going to burn in Hell for hypocrisy and self-righteousness • you are convinced that the voice of God is Charlton Heston • you are short-sighted • you are deep-down jealous of Bill Clinton's sex life! • you are angry that the cleaners lost your swastika arm band • you are lost in the middle of nowhere • you are going to talk about a man's record, talk about the whole record • you are one of them • you are not alone • you are one of those who would like to merge your work with earning a living, how do you go about doing it? This is the sort of question financial planning should address • you are right now compared to those doing what you want to do • you are going to pay for travelling from here to there • you are going to burn in Hell for hypocrisy and self-righteousness • you are frying fish on the beach • you are you're thefirst thing I think about and that's how the morning starts, it seems like everything I say and do is all about me being in love with you 24-7, you're the only thing that matters to me 24 hours girl, every day, seven long days a week I'm in heaven, heaven 24-7, you're the only train of thought on my one-track mind going ninety miles an hour baby all the time,

24-7, you're the only thing that matters to me 24 hours girl, every day, seven long days a week I'm in heaven, heaven 24-7, I'm in heaven 24-7 24 hours girl, every day seven long days a week I'm in heaven • you are skilled in network design and engineering • you are a communications specialist, you can earn a CCIP or CCIE, or you can get one of several specialty certificates to show you are competent in one particular area of Cisco Networking • you are expected to know everything there is to know when you walk through the door on the first day • you are allowed to drive any type of car that is manufactured

(cheating)

you are called, as you might very well be, to testify as a witness •
you are what the courts know as an "expert witness," entitled to
special fees • you are summoned to court • you are being baited
for a contradiction later on • you are asked a question that you
can't honestly answer by a mere "yes" or "no" say so and ask that
it be reworded • you are also sure it was this crash that first drew
your attention to these vehicles?" Her answer came quickly and
unthinkingly • you are simply weakening a system of justice that
protects you if you try to avoid testifying in court when you
possess valuable evidence • you are a good time manager? • you
are still not sure what area of study to choose, try our resources
to help you make this major choice • you are will help you foster
your best study setting • you are up to your ears in group projects,
here's how to avoid team work terrors and do well • you are a
focused student or a practicing procrastinator, good time
management is key • you are doing?" Adam demanded • you are
also entered to win $50,000 or a Porsche • you are hot! • you are
a sick, sick person! you think I could ever fall for some loser creep
in a lab coat? Some worthless slimeball who wants to control me
to boost his own pathetic ego? You're insane! Ben: I thought – Jill:
No! I don't care what you thought! Just get lost! Now! Ben: No, I
can fix this! I can go – Jill: Yes! Just go! Just go and leave us alone,
all right? You should just go and leave every one alone! Ben: Or…
or I could do that, yes • you are expending way too much time and
energy waiting for your man to mess up • you are so suspicious of
him 'cause you are slipping and falling onto a few penises your-
self • you are rewarding his faithfulness with suspicion and accu-
sation • you are a child of God • you are not living your own life
in a bold way – if you are hiding from your authentic self, afraid
to be who you really are, settling for less and settling for being
comfortable even though you are not fulfilled in what you are
doing with your life – then you are cheating the rest of us out of
the real you • you are in the world to heal the world • you are in

the space to heal the space • you are English • you are English by Graham John Francis de Sales Wheeler we're rapidly becoming the are • you are English • you are dimly aware that the royals have always been there and probably always will • you are an older northerner you may have a strange taste for tripe and onions • you are middle-class, you may vote for the liberal Democrats if you think of yourself as socially concerned • you are introduced to someone up to and including the Prime Minister, you can nowadays call them by their first name, unless you are in an officers' mess or the Garrick Club • you are a woman, you might go to the beach topless • you are not going to die of cholera or other third world diseases • you are not a farmer • you are a pedestrian and cars are stopped at a red light, you will fearlessly cross the street in front of them • you are middle-class, you may often holiday in France; if working-class, you'll probably prefer Spain or the Spanish islands • you are a Londoner • you are Jewish, you spend it with your family, give presents and put up a tree • you are told to vacate your office on the 7th floor, the management would remove your office address from that little sign in the lobby • you are deleted from the office • you are disputing the lease terms and you've decided to hang around another week – of course you are still up there, having a grand time • you are still around, it might decide to delete you permanently – by removing you physically • you are up there having a party • you are cheating yourself and your loved ones with phony excuses • you are asking for help and I hope I'll be able to give you some insight into your problem • you are still a virgin • you are in no position now to be committed to him or anyone else • you are destroying this relationship is because you don't feel that you deserve John • you are punishing yourself by making you even less worthy of a good relationship • you are and adult so you do it to yourself • you are ready to commit to John

(never going to fit everything in and oh! what about the "gaps")

you are using won't let you experience the full wonder of the design and text formatting • you are wrong or could do better in some particular • you are sober and able to string words together in a semi-coherent fashion • you are right, I shouldn't have come into work today – and I was reminded that I still haven't related the full sorry tale of the zealous religious commitment of my youth • you are so pretty, she would say • "you are kinda strange! Kinda strange!" Arnold Friend cried • "you are with Arnold Friend and don't you forget it! Maybe you better step out here," he said and this last was in a different voice • you are going to do is this: you are going to come out that door • "you are crazy," she muttered • you are coming out here • you are crazy, you • you are deaf, get a hearing aid, right? fix yourself up • you are close • you are now – inside your daddy's house – is nothing but a cardboard box I can knock down any time • you are better than them because not a one of them would have done this for you • you are "sorry" • you are mad! • you are awake and the last thing you think of before you go to bed, then he is really somebody special • you are the most beautiful and irresistible thing on earth and nothing can ever change that • you are going to get hurt is like living knowing that you are going to die • you are over the limit of limit characters • you are using someone else's computer and need to see what you saved last time you used your own machine, log on as if you were going to buy something and you will be able to access your saved wheelbarrow items • you are a first-timer, or a regular who wants to send stuff to a different address, go through the normal check-out and we'll get you sorted • you are going to pay big money for anything, make sure you get it checked before you buy! The second is to never buy anything based on looks alone ice cream for the eyes • you are given • you are interested in buying a 1969 Roadrunner in about two months, let me know • you are thinking "do you really want to know?"' Jennifer Schaefer, 34, lost her husband a year ago to cancer • you are flying without a net

• you are so different after something like this happens to you • you are about to be a part of an adventure, a family • you are having doubts • you are having any doubts • you are having any doubts, remember you are about to embark on a great adventure • you are thinking of/tell me if you love me now • you are fat • you are ugly • you are unpopular • you are not witty • you are not smart • you are ignorant • you are stupid • you are unpopular • you are nothing • you are fat • you are one of the crowd • you are a follower • you are a freak • you are a lah-hoo-ser • you are not sexy enough • you are retarded • you are unhappy • you are unsatisfied • you are not moving forward • you are not keeping up the pace • you are lagging behind • you are one step behind the rest • you are doing it all wrong • you are fat • you are not thin enough • you are too thin • you are lactose intolerant • you are iron deficient • you are far too dependant on drugs • you are bipolar • you are manic • you are not happy enough • you are not right • you are lagging behind • you are free • you are fat because you watch too much television • you are going to be a star one day • you are nothing • you are too fat • you are now suspecting what you are afraid to admit • you are sitting at the other corner of the kitchenette • you are here is you woke up alone, felt the dent in her pillow and followed the scent, sat down silently and she poured you a cup of coffee and sat in the sun and set to creating daytime, daydreams, why wake up? • you are now reading the newspaper, just like you are now • you are comparing her to God • you are not • you are dribbling into eternity • you are going too fast • you are likely to be eaten by a Grue • you are walking your dog on public land, you have to have them on a leash • you are stealing the content, making you a thief • you are "breaking your contract with the network" • you are ringing up my Slurpee

(feeling quite overwhelmed you must say)

you are a failure • you are able to divine how people are feeling about you • you are continually on trial to prove that your opinions and actions are correct • you are used to working full-time, being at home, much of the time alone with your newborn, is tough • you are feeling tired or overwhelmed • you are nursing your baby • you are finding this too difficult • you are in Columbus, Ohio • you are a sadist who just wants to read it and laugh hysterically at me • you are utterly incapable of feeling or understanding what you have been doing to me for so long • you are not fit to feel or capable of retaining • you are both • you are drawn to me, you cannot help but come near • you are frightened, I can hear it in your breath • you are not to blame • you are there, you have reached your peak • you are greeted by talking androids, noisy factory equipment and high tech sights and sound • you are about ready to jump out of your skin • you are sick of all this suspicion and foolishness • you are ill and he is good and your illness is infectious for him • you are more yourself • you are lightheaded! You were delirious when you did all this! For a moment Raskolnikov felt everything going round • you are never going to fit everything in and oh! what about the "gaps" • you are a concrete person so I'm going to figure that you wouldn't mind a pre-planned lesson for your son • you are going to give him a choice in some of the subjects he will study • you are such a dick to me • you are turned away another wound that I'd take back if I could fill your heart just once and then I'd take you now where we could live again faces in disguise not a trace of desire cold faces in disguise not a trace of desire go face the day go and see new things go face the day but you'll remember me • you are keeping from yourself, which is the truth of what a beautiful person you are • you are likely to be living through, tremendous awareness is necessary • you are not figuring out that these are indeed amazing moments of your life, you are not paying attention • you are going too fast, or not able to focus, or overwhelmed with potential

• you are faced with the challenges that arrive on that level • you are unlikely ever to be freed from the task of having to establish yourself as an individual • you are strange or unacceptable • you are now in a position to see that it wasn't coming from anyplace but you • you are not just firm in your convictions, but rather steadfastly devoted to what you know to be true • you are working through and working on is located on the emotional level • you are sometimes inclined to think • you are not to blame for the insensitive actions of others, though you have a lot of control over how you respond to them • you are not already on the case • you are about to have that need become a possibility – if you will take advantage of it • you are in an extended phase of working out your highest aspirations • you are concerned • you are the mad poet! • you are offended by strong language or subject matter then do not go any further

(black, all you can do is pray for the person at the centre of the next blatant misdeed that draws national attention)

you are not the praying sort, just think • you are living in a country that has taken a stand with the Palestinian and against Israel and you can be certain judgment is soon coming • you are lost and without hope and in bondage to your own fantasy • you are an over-overcomer • you are persistent • you are asked to join in a Stargate or ritual meditation on a global basis • you are thinking about it • you are in poverty and believe it is better to pray for understanding • you are in need and you will not be able to get out of it • you are an over-spender • you are doing the ritual using the soul of a deceased person, but why didn't you first purify the soul-body first? • you are just standing there under the black flag with all those bloodstains on you

(still a virgin)

"you are evil," I cried, laughing too • you are publishing today •
you are recycling this article • you are still a virgin? • you are preg-
nant • you are ready to have sex is you! Here are some questions
you can ask yourself to help determine if you are ready: does
having sex support your personal values and goals? Do you
understand and accept the emotional risks of having sex? Are you
ready to protect yourself and your partner from physical risks,
like infections and pregnancy? Do you feel pressured to have sex
by your partner or peers? Are you ready to talk openly about sex
with your partner? Do you care about and trust your partner?
When to have sex is a personal choice • you are about – your
health, education and career goals, relationships with other
people and your feelings about yourself • you are not a teen • you
are in immediate danger go to a friend's house invite friends over
make a phone call to a caring adult you are in charge of you • you
are the only one in the world who has the right to say who will
touch your body • you are letting him/her know that your body is
not up for grabs • you are alone in a room with someone who
makes you feel uneasy, leave the room immediately • you are still
a virgin • you are having trouble launching the online service
console on your PC there are a few things you can try • you are
using Windows 95 or 98 and are happy that your screen can
handle the appropriate resolution, please refer to the following
process to change your screen settings • you are not sure whether
your screen can handle the appropriate resolution, please give
our technical support team a call • you are happy with the changes
click "'yes'" and you can then close the display properties and
control panel screens • you are not able to use online service at
present • you are having a problem with your global key code,
don't forget it's case sensitive and the last character is a letter • you
are having a problem with your password or passcode, please call
us • you are still having problems launching our online service
console, call us • you are a woman and have wandered onto this

page by mistake, read no further! The following information is intended for your husband only • you are positive she's guilty, consider planting evidence of wrongdoing in her room, such as a dirty magazine or a contraceptive product, in order to "prompt" her admission of guilt • you are doing is for her own good and that under no circumstances is she to mention the "finger test" to anyone but you • you are saving her from a ruined life and also improving the soundness of your own sleep • you are Italian! • you are Italian! If your brother can have three girlfriends all sleep over at the same time, but your sister, who is 19, has to be in bed by 7 pm – you are Italian! As a first generation Italo-Canadian male, I find no fault in this particular statement • you are currently in therapy over recurring nightmares about disciplinary items such as leather belts and wooden spoons, you are Italian! This is grossly false • you are Italian! We may change the sofa but we always reuse the plastic covers • you are Italian! I must agree with this one • you are Italian! Yeah • you are Italian! OK • you are Italian! Absolutely correct • you are Italian! Wrong • you are Italian! Sorry, I'm not able to verify that one because I can't speak and type at the same time • you are Italian! Wrong again! See what I mean • you are Italian! To prove how incorrect this statement is, here is a list of pictures on the walls at home • you are Italian! *Basta!* Canadian weddings? Give me a break • you are Italian! Thank God in heaven that's true! If your dad still has his suit from his communion in his closet and decides to wear it to a formal function • you are Italian! Look • you are Italian! This is truly an insult • you are Italian! Where did you dig up this pseudo-Italian stuff? Real fear was to get slapped on the side of the head with the palm of the hand • you are Italian! That's really pushing the envelope • you are Italian! Silvestro the gimp or Felice the rabble rouser are perfectly easy ways to differentiate people • you are willing to miss the birth of your child due to a soccer game during the World Cup • you are Italian! Hey, a kid can be born every nine months • you are a girl of 16 and you are seen with a guy by anyone in your family and they ask you if you are going to get married anytime soon • you are Italian! Come on • you are 35 years old, still live at home, still have your mom cook, clean for you and you still have the balls to bitch about having to eat "pasta fazool" for dinner again • you are Italian! Well, I'm over 35 and I live at home … Let's be logical

(a fine piece of work)

you are not an exception • you are done with that piece • you are
only supposed to upload a piece when you are done with it • you
are already here • you are working on to see if what you think the
notes are is the same as what someone else thinks it never hurts
to double-check your transcriptions with multiple sources so you
get all the notes/chords correct • you are at all interested in
computing away from your desktop, you need this book • you are
better off with Blair • you are certifying that you are over the age
of 18; please read our disclaimer • you are lucky, you might
manage it • you are new to this site, we strongly recommend that
you visit our info page • you are here > user rave page 1 • you are
going to totally take over the market, forget Sausage Software's
Hot Dog and Allaire's Homesite! Great great software • you are
crazy giving it away for free! But I hope you'll be crazy for a long
time • you are here" • you are here • you are equipped like a pro
with a few top-quality knives that you love using will serve you
better than a wide variety of different ones • you are chopping
large amounts • you are thinking about a road ride this weekend
• you are like most cyclists you are less fit and heavier than you are
at any other time of the year • you are like me you start getting
anxious just looking at your bike • you are flexing your ankle
pushing your foot down at the bottom of you pedal stroke or
mashing on your pedal • you are riding relaxed • you are no different
than everyone else who loves the sport of cycling

(a second string guy, so you have to prepare like you are a starter)

you are in serious trouble • you are constantly being evaluated • you are the committee • you are living strong • you are in the heat of the battle • you are a very exciting player to watch • you are in the profit straight away! • you are in at the start • you are giving 110 percent • you are supporting cancer survivors • you are a baller • you are a second-string guy, so you have to prepare like you are a starter • you are a little small – I'd suggest working out • you are willing to learn • you are willing to work hard for something • you are going to be on the field • you are still playing football no matter what position you are playing • you are on bad terms with your head coach but that should never dictate how you play, how your prepare • you are playing a high school team or a college team, you just have to go out there and show you are the better man • you are gonna get it now, huh? If Shaq and I go up for a rebound and I want that rebound with all of my heart and Shaq couldn't care less if he got it, Shaq's still going to get that rebound • you are fully committed to doing what's necessary to reach your goal • you are open to receiving candid feedback, even if it addresses your contributions to the problem • you are the biggest mouth on the team • you are talking about multi-line scoring and firing on all cylinders then no one in the league does that better than the Avalanche, with 11 players contributing in double digit scoring • you are still my hero and would you please sign my football card of you? Mom says she can't afford Christmas presents for us, so your autograph would sort of be like my Christmas • you are letting down your teammates – you couldn't begin to carry Jerry Rice's jockstrap! • you are a disgrace to your team, your sport and your country • you are not a first-round pick • you are probably not going to get those opportunities again until a coach comes along that believes in you and believes you can play • you are going to have that label put on you for the rest of your career • you are a fifth-string guy and there will always be better competition • you are in serious trouble • you are constantly being evaluated • you are

271

playing catch on the sidelines • you are new to the sport, you need to learn a few things about the world's fastest game • you are cut from the team • you are definitely playing in the prairie provinces now • you are reading these words – I'm "editing" you – trying to induce a change in your verbal image of the world, your own "wikipedia" • you are likely to struggle with it, changing your opinion many times and trying to arrange your epistemological web into a satisfactory equilibrium • you are constantly coming across sentences rather like this: "A letter from Gussie Fink-Nottle, newt-fancier from Kent, says that the spotted newt can hybridize with the striped newt, but not the solid newt" • you are more likely to qualify if you weren't a low-wage, undocumented, or part-time worker in the first place – but this was always more or less so; what's changed now, Shillington argues, is that the program is now actively regressive in the way it redistributes wealth amongst workers • you are not paranoid if they actually hate you ... and it's easy for an Albertan to conclude that in Alberta – as both a real polity and as a bogeyman of the imagination – but this has been the only real issue in the last few federal elections • you are thinking of spending a protest vote on the Green Party – especially on the grounds that you'd like them to have campaign funding to "promote their ideas" • you are afraid the conservatives will sell out to American values • you are thinking that Michael Ignatieff has a future in Canadian politics despite starting out on the wrong foot with the Ukrainians • you are like me and are already getting a little bored with online prediction markets • you are stuck in a low income bracket • you are up at 6 am to water the rink • you are going to work until you die • you are going out shopping, looking for a hockey sweater, maybe • you are going to go out and stand in line to get into a store early, whose jersey do you absolutely have to have? • you are depriving some poor village of its idiot • you are a not just a band mom, but a hockey mom! • you are already there • you are not going to be in the league • you

272

are not good enough • you are hoping your son makes the NHL – its not likely, don't attend the draft • you are answering a question from the media, or run into someone in the grocery store who tells you you are not good enough, or tells you you'll end up just the same way everybody else did and there is going to be a point where you start to believe it • you are in serious trouble • you are constantly being evaluated • you are not going to have much fun with this game • you are playing like you're trying to protect a lead that you don't have • you are in a backup role • you are out of luck

(done with that piece)

you are planning to spend at least one solid day of your Thanksgiving weekend updating your game AI site • you are more likely to simulate a problem than to actually solve it • you are doing – but it looks great • you are too busy debugging a piece of code • you are too busy debugging a piece of code • you are walking down the street • you are sitting in a bar and think "nice texture map" as you look at the wood grain on the table • you are virtually unaffected by the caffeine in your favourite drinks • you are satisfied! • you are an actor portraying a two-year-old • you are either still in, or have recently graduated from college • you are still in school, then your most up-to-date information is fine • you are right-handed, fill the right-hand panel first, then move to the panel on the left and continue your writing • you are using a sliding, three-layered chalkboard, fill the middle board first, then push it up and pull the front board down • you are modifying a drawing, use dotted lines or some other technique to show changes • you are not sure of the answer, ask your students • you are right-handed, so view isn't blocked • you are wearing – one look at the distinctive swoosh on the side tells everyone who's got you branded • you are carrying – ah, you are a Starbucks woman! Your T-shirt with the distinctive champion "C" on the sleeve, the blue jeans with the prominent Levi's rivets, the watch with the hey-this-certifies-I-made-it icon on the face, your fountain pen with the maker's symbol crafted into the end • you are going to read and respond to first – and whose you are going to send to the trash unread? The answer: personal branding • you are really smart, you figure out how to distinguish yourself from all the other very smart people walking around with $1,500 suits, high-powered laptops and well-polished resumes • you are really smart, you figure out what it takes to create a distinctive role for yourself – you create a message and a strategy to promote the brand called you • you are going to think of yourself differently! (You're not an "employee" of General Motors, you are not a "staffer" at General

Mills, you are not a "worker" at General Electric or a "human resource" at General Dynamics – ooops, it's gone!) • you are not confined by your job description • you are a brand • you are going to be a brand, you've got to become relentlessly focused on what you do that adds value, that you are proud of and most important, that you can shamelessly take credit for • you are General Motors, Ford, or Chrysler, that usually means a full flight of TV and print ads designed to get billions of "impressions" of your brand in front of the consuming public • you are brand you, you've got the same need for visibility – but no budget to buy it • you are a better writer than you are a teacher, try contributing a column or an opinion piece to your local newspaper • you are a better talker than you are teacher or writer, try to get yourself on a panel discussion at a conference or sign up to make a presentation at a workshop • you are promoting brand you, everything you do – and everything you choose not to do – communicates the value and character of the brand • you are thinking like brand you, you don't need org-chart authority to be a leader • you are a leader • you are not spending at least 70 percent of your time working on projects, creating projects or organizing your apparently mundane tasks into projects, you are sadly living in the past • you are learning, growing, building relationships and delivering great results, it's good for you and it's great for the company • you are treating your résumé as if it's a marketing brochure, you've learned the first lesson of free agency • you are doing today, there are four things you've got to measure yourself against • you are a brand • you are in charge of your brand • you are getting that first kiss when you get home and the perfect vision of a quilt pops into your head • you are going so that you won't hear "Oh no, not another quiltshow!" • you are going to a quilt show! • you are trying to sketch the complex design in the tile floor because it'd make a neat quilt design!! • you are making travel plans and one of your first thoughts is if there are any must-see quilting stores within a 100-mile radius of your destination • you are _married_ to a quilter when picking snippets of cloth and thread off of each other goes unnoticed and becomes a habitual behaviour, similar to the grooming activities of primates • you are married to a _modern_ quilter when your electronic mailbox gets filled with 50 messages every day and it's _all_ related to quilting • you are married to the _right_ quilter when the joy that he/she gets from the quilting art, coupled with the beauty of the objects that he/she creates, makes the "quilter's eye," the snippets, the "stash," the overflowing e-mail, the visiting of fabric stores on vacations and all of the other "quilters' anomalies" extremely worthwhile • you are getting a manicure, haircut, whatever and you check out the floor and ask if they have any extra floor tiles because the pattern would make a great quilt • you are removing some "small" items from your closet and run across a sundress you wore on your honeymoon • you are thinking to yourself, give it away? Huh! That's cotton! • you are having for dinner tonight! Pam N • you are going to make your supervisor a quilt • you are thinking of buying • you are supposedly taking notes in a meeting • you are wearing a thimble on your finger – or worse yet, drop your thimble into the toilet – oh yuck! Because you forgot you had it on • you are travelling through the America West terminal in Phoenix, Arizona and you are fascinated by the pattern in the carpet and sit in the gate area and chart it out on grid paper that you just happen to have in your briefcase! • you are in a strange city and spot a quilt store, you almost cause an accident trying to do a U-turn • you are flying over the neat and orderly farms in the midwest and all you can see is 9 patch blocks alfalfa goes one way, corn another, wheat a third, etc. • you are talking in code all the time, can you translate that to "English?" • you are sick or leaving! • you are designing your next quilt and must get up to put it on paper • you are on vacation and it's no fun until you find at least one fabric store • you are out in the hallway of your motel tracing the pattern of the wallpaper because it would make a good quilting design • you are a quilter, even though you've never said a word about it! • you are in charge of for work find you in the hotel room during small groups with the bernina you sneaked in, sewing strips for the 9-patch exchange you signed up for on Q-exchange! • you are in the lobby hand-quilting your border exchange project! • you are sitting in a courtroom as a prospective juror and all you can think about is that the ceiling mouldings would make a *great* border quilting pattern • you are preparing a meal for your 4-year-old and you start daydreaming • you are afraid it will get on your work

(deep blue)

you are feeling • you are getting too stressed • you are not a money
magnet • you are interested in learning about the differences
between Chinese and American educational systems • you are
feeling particularly artistic so maybe you should paint a fish • you
are familiar with many TV personalities and celebrities • you are
not afraid of upsetting the boys • you are used to not believing in
most of what you read or hear – people are supposed to "say what
they mean" or remain silent • you are a single or divorced parent,
even a mother who has never wanted to marry or live with the
father of her children • you are accustomed to taking care of the
poor, sick and disabled • you are good at it • you are a pedestrian,
you cross streets on the appropriate walkways when there is a
green light for pedestrians • you are a blue pool shark • you are a
girl, of course; expect to be treated like a novelty and have to fend
off questions about what you are painting and whether or not
you'd like to be in their painting competition • you are bored of
just having black nails and want something different • you are
rooted in place • you are overcome with remorse

(entirely happy with your poem)

you are entirely happy with your poem • you are not happy then
there is no charge and your deposit is returned • you are totally
satisfied with the outcome • you are a man • you are a little
confused • you are entirely happy with your poem • you are not
happy then there is no charge and your deposit is returned • you
are totally satisfied with the outcome • "… you are wonderful"
Lori • you are a wonderful and very gifted person • you are entirely
happy with your poem • you are not happy then there is no charge
and your deposit is returned • you are totally satisfied with the
outcome • you are far from home • you are fed up with suitcase
life and sleeping on your own • you are fed up with airline food
and feeling half dead, half alive • you are entirely happy with your
poem • you are not happy then there is no charge and your deposit
is returned • you are totally satisfied with the outcome • you are
near • you are really kind and generous and would sacrifice
anything for me, you are the solid branch, of our new-found
family tree • you are the best! • you are entirely happy with your
poem • you are not happy then there is no charge and your deposit
is returned • you are totally satisfied with the outcome • you are
my last hope for a man and I'm your mid-life crisis, we're just
doing the best we can! But you can never sit still, you are always
out mowing the grass, not that it's really hard work, because you
just sit on your big fat ass • you are a world champion snorer, boy,
you can really snore! In fact, you've sawn so many logs, they litter
our forest floor! We have two lovely daughters, they are both
growing and oh so fast, but we won't buy that shotgun just yet,
we'll just warn them about parked cars! We've got our six dogs
and Brutus is our Great Dane, you'd better watch his whip action,
that tail can cause a lot of pain • you are the most loving man, I
have ever known in my life and I am so very, very happy, to be with
you as your wife • you are much more than a husband, Mike, you
are like my very best friend and it is hard to wrap all that up, as
these words come to an end • you are entirely happy with your

poem • you are not happy then there is no charge and your deposit is returned • you are totally satisfied with the outcome • you are cute • you are more than that to me • you are cute • you are more than that to me • you are more than welcome to publish the poem on your site – after all u wrote it! But I would appreciate it if you could leave out my story altogether as now that I've told all my friends about your site, there are some of whom I wouldn't like to know about this • you are entirely happy with your poem • you are not happy then there is no charge and your deposit is returned • you are totally satisfied with the outcome • you are going to be a daddy, happy anniversary, happy Father's Day! • you are entirely happy with your poem • you are not happy then there is no charge and your deposit is returned • you are totally satisfied with the outcome • you are on a roll • you are entirely happy with your poem • you are not happy then there is no charge and your deposit is returned • you are totally satisfied with the outcome • "… you are wonderful" Lori • you are awesome!!! I like it thank you very much • you are entirely happy with your poem • you are not happy then there is no charge and your deposit is returned • you are totally satisfied with the outcome • you are so full of charisma and grace

As one knows without saying, we do not write anymore.
– Friedrich Kittler

afterword

We have more moral, political, and historical wisdom than we know how to reduce into practice; we have more scientific and economical knowledge than can be accomodated to the just distribution of the produce which it multiplies. The poetry in these systems of thought is concealed by the accumulation of facts and calculating processes.... We want the creative faculty to imagine that which we know; we want the generous impulse to create that which we imagine; we want the poetry of life.

– Percy Bysshe Shelley, *Defence of Poetry*

You are now at the end of the book.

The first version of the poem at the *other* end of this book, "apostrophe (ninety-four)," was written by Bill in 1993, and first appeared in the Poetics issue of *SinOverTan*, our small-press poetry zine. We both have a long-standing fascination with the catalogue poem, especially its penchant for listing and itemizing. The catalogue poem has been with us at least since Homer's *Iliad* went on (at length, of course) about the "chiefs and princes of the Danaans" and the 1186 ships they brought to sack Troy; it has twisted and turned its way through poems sacred and profane ever since.

The catalogue is a form that struggles with excess. Its job is to be reductive, to squeeze all of the possibilities that a world of information has to offer into a definitive set – not just *the* Greeks, but *these* Greeks. Its poetic effect, however, is the exact opposite. A catalogue opens up a poem to the threat of a surfeit of information, felt most keenly when the reader wonders, politely, *"How long can this go on?"*

It can, in fact, go on for a very long time. Forever, really. In 1993, when the full implications of the nascent World Wide Web were only beginning to occur to us, the catalogue and its paradoxical struggles were already becoming the forum for addressing the fear that we are producing text at a rate beyond our collective ability to read it. David Filo and Jerry Yang began Yahoo! in 1994 as an attempt to keep track of their favourite sites; before long, they were spending more time updating their catalogue than they were on their doctoral dissertations. (We know all about that one, too). When faced with an infinitude of text, the choice of what to read – or write, for that matter – is both vital and largely arbitrary.

As a figure of speech, apostrophe implicates the reader in the production of excess information. Barbara Johnson, in an essay which inspired the original poem, writes that apostrophe is "almost synonymous with the lyric voice." Shelley's address – "O wild West Wind" – is also addressing the reader: *you* are the wild West Wind. As Johnson notes, this is a complex gesture. You, the reader, are now both responsible for the poem and yet somehow being spoken for, by a poet, of all people. It is this tension between responsibility and alienation that *apostrophe* attempts to capture.

Despite the fact that we came up with the idea while sitting at a bar, our decision to automate the poem seemed logical: *apostrophe* is all about address, and so is the Web. The apostrophe engine (now housed at apostropheengine.ca), as we named the program itself, is fairly simple. Bill's original poem became a kind of interface, with each of the lines as a hyperlink.

When a reader/writer clicks on a line of the digital version of the poem, it is submitted to a search engine, which returns a list of pages. The apostrophe engine then spawns virtual robots that work their way through the list, scraping the pages for phrases beginning with "you are" and ending in a period. The robots stop after collecting a set number of phrases or working through a limited number of pages, whichever happens first. The apostrophe engine records and spruces up the phrases that the robots have collected, stripping away most HTML tags and other anomalies, then compiles the results and presents them as a new poem, with the original line as its title ... and each new line as another hyperlink. At any given time, the online version of the poem is potentially as large as the Web itself.

We were perfectly willing to concede failure if the results were unimpressive, but the apostrophe engine produces surprising, charged and often enigmatic texts. We appreciate the lack of affect in the results; they are a metonymic slide through the vernacular of the Web. The etymological roots of "apostrophe" derive from the Greek verb "to turn away" or "to turn aside," and that's exactly what the engine does, performing a digital *détournement* that liberates language from one context in order to tease out other entanglements. Even when the program encounters anomalous diction or badly coded web pages, it still produces a wealth of uncanny results.

apostrophe, it should be noted, makes no claims to procedural purity. When Racter's *The Policeman's Beard is Half-Constructed* (the self-described "first book ever written by a computer") appeared in 1984, it came with provocative introductory claims of being "completely unedited," insisting that it produced prose that was "in no way contingent upon the human experience," though consensus now is that the book was generated with the help of a set of templates not included with the commercial version of the program. Ultimately, tying the merits of Racter's writing to the lack of human agency involved in its production has proved distracting; there is a sense among Racter's critics and detractors that the writing's worth can be challenged merely by debunking Racter's programmers, Bill Chamberlain and Thomas Etter.

We suspect that this line of critique is part of a larger anxiety about the role of the artist's creativity in the production of art, an anxiety Racter's programmers were all too willing to provoke, but one that we do not share. We are happy to point out that *apostrophe* is a tainted text, with none of Racter's dubious innocence. The apostrophe engine has meddled with the writing of others, and we in turn have done the same with its writing. We were fortunate. The engine provided us with an embarrassment of riches, an abundance of raw material, beautiful and banal at once and by turns. It was our pleasure and responsibility to be its first, most skeptical readers.

Like most hopeful monsters, the apostrophe engine will likely be the source of its own demise. We speculated from the outset that once sections of the book began to appear online, the engine would begin to cannibalize itself, returning its own results before other, less likely matches. And we were right (see "a refutation of the Special Theory of Relativity" for an example). This process has been accelerated by the increasing sophistication of engine technologies; after all, the results of the apostrophe engine only work as poetry to the extent that search engines don't succeed at their job. Play with it while you can; childhood is almost over.

notes and
acknowledgements

Portions of *apostrophe* have appeared in *Against Expression: An Anthology of Conceptual Writing, The Boston Review, Carnival: A Scream in High Park Reader, The Common Sky: Canadian Writers Against the War, filling Station, Matrix, New American Poetry, Object, Saints of Hysteria: A Half-Century of Collaborative American Poetry, SinOverTan, Taddle Creek* and *The Whitewall Review*. A section of *apostrophe* was published by Housepress.

Bill and Darren would like to thank David Antin, derek beaulieu, Charles Bernstein, Daccia Bloomfield, Christian Bök, Brian Joseph Davis, Darren O'Donnell, Johanna Drucker, Craig Dworkin, Neil Hennessey, Jesse Huisken, Rob Fitterman, Kenny Goldsmith, Sarah Kenvyn, Mishann Lau, Jason LeHeup, Michael Holmes, Robert Kroetsch, Karen Mac Cormack, Steve McCaffery, Katherine Parrish, Marjorie Perloff, Angela Rawlings, Kim Rosenfield, Emily Schultz, Michael Snow, Brian Kim Stefans, Steve Venright and Alana Wilcox for their support of the project. We'd also like to thank all of those who wrote in the second person. We'd be nothing without you.

Several of the pieces in the Appendix were generated by Angela Rawlings; a version of "deep blue" was generated at the request of Christian Bök, who read it at the memorial of the painter Lynn Donoghue.

The oldest sections of *apostrophe* – (home by the sea), (deftly turned phrase), (driving a gas-guzzling '71 Impala), (a festering war wound incurred in a skirmish between the US and Canada over rights to a pig farm), (a case of halitosis, gingivitis, dandruff and split ends) and (the wrong answer on the multiple choice section of the LSAT), in that order – were generated on April 18, 2001, using AltaVista as the source of searches.

The majority of the pieces in "layer two" were generated between September 9, 2002 and October 2, 2002, with Google as the source. Pieces marked with an asterisk (*) originally returned no results. The pieces that appear under asterisked titles in this book were generated on February 27, 2006. Likewise, pieces marked with a dagger (†) are alternate versions of earlier pieces that we chose to rerun in February 2006 for a variety of reasons. The difference in their content and syntax reflects the changing nature of the Web itself.

ECW PRESS
ecwpress.com

Published by ECW Press
2120 Queen Street East, Suite 200,
Toronto, Ontario, Canada M4E 1E2

Editor: Michael Holmes / a misFit book
Cover: Bill Kennedy
Typesetting: Darren Wershler-Henry and Bill Kennedy
Printing: Marquis Imprimeur
This book is set in Minion and Quay Sans

DISTRIBUTION
Canada: Jaguar Book Group,
100 Armstrong Ave., Georgetown, ON L7G 5S4

United States: Independent Book Publishers Group,
814 North Franklin Street, Chicago, Il, USA, 60610

PRINTED AND BOUND IN CANADA